T0294193

Also available at all good book stores

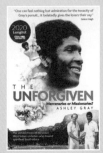

9781785315329

9781785317330

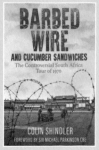

9781785316340

9781908051929

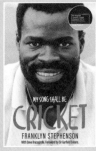

9781785315398

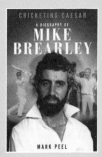

9781785316623

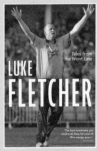

9781785316876

9781785316630

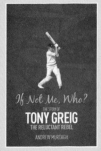

9781785316418

Sachin and Azhar
at Cape Town

ABHISHEK MUKHERJEE
AND ARUNABHA SENGUPTA

Sachin *and* Azhar *at Cape Town*

Indian and South African Cricket Through the Prism of a Partnership

Foreword by Harsha Bhogle

First published by Pitch Publishing, 2021

Pitch Publishing
A2 Yeoman Gate
Yeoman Way
Worthing
Sussex
BN13 3QZ
www.pitchpublishing.co.uk
info@pitchpublishing.co.uk

A CIP catalogue record is available for this book
from the British Library.

ISBN 978 1 78531 819 1

Typesetting and origination by Pitch Publishing

Printed and bound in India by Replika Press Pvt. Ltd.

Contents

TO

The protagonists

Nelson Mandela

Sachin Tendulkar

Mohammad Azharuddin

Acknowledgements

THE AUTHORS would like to start by profusely thanking the late Clive Rice for the enormous amount of time spent in providing very candid interviews a few years ago, much of which has been invaluable for this book.

Dilip Vengsarkar was obliging and forthcoming in sharing his valuable thoughts and experiences.

Dennis Amiss was generous with his time in sharing his observations about the game.

Lance Klusener and Paul Adams, members of the 1996/97 South African side, went out of their way to help us with their recollections and insights.

Dodda Ganesh, a member of the 1996/97 Indian side, was similarly very accommodating in sharing his views.

Harsha Bhogle not only provided the splendid introduction in which he captured the essence of the book as concisely as only he could, he also proved extremely perceptive in immediately grasping the offbeat idea and was always full of encouragement and enthusiasm.

Senior journalists Vijay Lokapally and G. Viswanath helped immensely by sharing their memories. Chandresh Narayan deserves a special mention for the outstanding leads he provided.

B. Sreeram, or Wisden Sreeram as he is known in some circles, was as ever an asset in fact checking and also finding the elusive bits of information about the match that had been lost to all but his resourceful self in the last 24 years.

The extraordinary thoroughness of Dean Rockett's brilliant editing left the authors spellbound.

Maha, the inimitable artist, was incredible as usual with her prompt and high-quality artwork.

Mayukh Ghosh, with his suggestions of cricket literature, and Sumit Ganguly, with his immaculate research into old dusty scorebooks, provided prodigious help.

Jayanta Kumar Pal, Suvasree Basu and Ratnabali Sengupta helped out with the photographs taken in South Africa.

A few personal notes:
Arunabha would like to thank Paddy Briggs for volunteering to share his own research into the isolation years. He would also like to thank Stephen Chalke and Tony Ring for remaining the constant, interested well-wishers.

This being Abhishek's first half-book (or halfth first book), his list is longer. He would like to thank his mother for unsuspectingly introducing him to cricket, his father for that first cricket bat, his brother for relinquishing rights of the television remote control during live cricket; and Koi, the remarkably perceptive canine.

He would also like to thank Prodipto-*da*, Shakuntala, and Tanmay for being there through highs and lows; and Rituparna, for being a healthy influence.

And finally, his daughter who, for some reason, believes in him.

Pre-Match Presentation
(Introduction)
by
HARSHA BHOGLE

THE SOUTHERN tip of Africa. A land and a people that were distinct from the rest of the continent. White and black inhabited the place but the two hardly met. I only knew South Africa by one word. Apartheid. It was reprehensible, it was brutal, it was inhuman and so everything we saw about the land that nature was generous with, was through one prism. We knew about their cricket players playing in England and of Basil D'Oliveira, we knew the odd tennis player, we knew of diamonds and we knew of Johannesburg through the picture that Alan Paton had painted in *Cry, The Beloved Country*. It was a large city where bad things happened.

And of course we knew of the Gandhi connection and the incident on the train at Pietermaritzburg. The Congress Party, and so India, was close to the African National Congress and so when, under the weight of international condemnation, South Africa began opening up, we in India began to play a central role. South Africa was re-admitted to the ICC and within a week, a long time in India but a mere twinkling of an eye elsewhere, a team was flying out to India.

It was 1991, we had met Ali Bacher in Sharjah and he had introduced us to names in South African cricket. We had heard of Rice and Wessels and Donald and Cook and a bit of the older Kirsten brother but little else. The period between that great side of 1969 that beat Australia 4-0 and the team that was flying out was restricted to snippets of the rebel tours in a non-internet era.

Just a year later, some of us were flying into Johannesburg. We had no visas because there were still no diplomatic ties. We hadn't heard of the protea and the rand was the answer to a quiz question. It was an eye-opener. South Africa were a powerful but diffident cricket team who had to rely on Wessels to tell them what Test cricket was all about. When Wessels hit Kapil Dev on the foot in retaliation to his running out of Kirsten who was constantly outside his crease before the bowler bowled, Ali Bacher ensured that no footage was visible. Nothing could go wrong on that tour.

But you were never too far from politics. We were introduced to harrowing tales of the apartheid era, there was a protest in East London and when there was a reception in Bloemfontein, the heart of apartheid itself, we were told it was the largest collection of non-whites in the Town Hall! It was, of course, the Friendship Tour and a plaque still stands in Durban, opened by the youngest player on either side, Jonty Rhodes and Sachin Tendulkar. Soon Jonty was to run Sachin out, the first decision made by a replay umpire!

The cricket was tepid and the last Test excruciatingly boring. But the memories were good. To see a nation wake up is always special.

By the time India returned in 1996/97, South African cricket had shaken off its diffidence and was planting the seeds of two decades of outstanding performance. Mandela was in power and he was a compassionate leader, having ensured that South Africa hadn't gone the way of its beautiful neighbour Zimbabwe. The Rugby World Cup had played a big part in bringing people together, even if on the surface, and the rand was still relatively strong. On the field though, fine players were blooming. In the four years since India had visited, South Africa had unearthed Kallis, Pollock, Gary Kirsten, Cullinan, Gibbs and Klusener. It was as good a side as any in world cricket in such a short while.

India had regressed. The captaincy was changing hands, dark thoughts had started surfacing, openers had vanished, Srinath was at his peak and Prasad had appeared but that was it and the youngsters soon to set the world alight were mere buds. We feared the worst after the disaster on the trampoline at Durban.

Then that partnership happened. We had seen glimpses of it in an Azhar blitzkrieg at the Eden Gardens but we were unprepared for what followed. It didn't change the result but Tendulkar and Azharuddin, already no longer the best of friends, lit up a series and produced batsmanship that had few things to rival it till Sehwag arrived. I am fascinated by the idea of writing a social and cricketing treatise around one period of play. Far too often, we who cover cricket, don't place it in the perspective of a wider world. If anything, our vision has narrowed. Society and politics might seem distant neighbours of sport but in reality they are close cousins and nowhere is this more visible than in South Africa, the setting that two cricket lovers with a view of the world beyond cricket, have chosen to place this book in. It was the place to be in the nineties; cricket started with hope and ended in brief despair but it was at all times a mirror to a ravaged society looking for sustenance.

Arunabha and Abhishek, the numbers men with a flair for words, sensitive, history-loving writers, have attempted a mammoth task and in doing so look at South African cricket in a larger context. If anything, the game there has hollowed since but only the future can tell us if this was the necessary weeding out of one culture and the planting of another.

South Africa was the country to watch through the nineties. You can watch it in this book.

Pitch Inspection

THE STACK of books lies on the table. Each volume tantalisingly inviting. Each one incredibly difficult to procure in India.

The world, for all its pretensions of having become a global village, is still divided according to geographical regions and the corresponding ease and cumbrousness of logistics. Distribution of cricket books varies vastly from the West (Europe and United States) to Australia to India to South Africa. Unless of course we are talking about the ghosted – and often ghastly – autobiographies of superstars.

Among the pile are a number of volumes by Stephen Chalke, One More Run; Bob Appleyard: No Coward Soul; Geoffrey Howard: At the Heart of English Cricket. *There is* The West Indies at Lord's *by Alan Ross, a brace of Gerald Brodribbs, a David Foot. A couple of old tour books by Percy Fender.*

And then there is Alletson's Innings *by John Arlott.*

It is Arunabha's once-in-a-blue-moon visit to India, now that he has grown his expat roots in Amsterdam. The books are some of the items checked off the long wish-list of Abhishek, whatever could be crammed into a cabin luggage without tilting the scales or bursting at the seams. One cannot, of course, take chances with the airlines misplacing the check-in bags. That has happened too many times for us to gamble with such invaluable cricket books.

The proximity to England allows Arunabha to be the closest possible approximation of Santa for Abhishek and other cricket-book connoisseurs in India. Back in Amsterdam, his own collection eats up living space and bank balance on a daily and dangerous basis.

Abhishek picks up the last-named volume.

AM: *Alletson's Innings.* Nottinghamshire vs Sussex at Hove, 1911. Alletson walked out to bat at 185/7 in the second innings, Notts ahead by just nine runs. By lunch he was 47 not out, scored in 50 minutes, Nottinghamshire on 260/9. And then came the storm.

AS: Alletson supposedly asked his captain, A.O. Jones, how he should approach his innings after resumption. Jones waved him off, saying it didn't matter what he did. 'Then I'm not half going to give [Tim] Killick some stick,' Alletson supposedly said. Then it happened. 142 in 40 minutes.

AM: And to think that he was known as a blocker.

Let's not forget his bowling skills too. For years he had been trying to perfect the ultimate magic ball – the finger-spun leg break. He used to practise on this for hours, his father standing behind the stumps to throw the ball back to him. It took him six years to use it in a competitive match.

It was his sixth season and he had five fifties in 105 innings. And now he went out and scored 142 out of 152 for the tenth wicket. 115 off seven overs.

AS: Thirty-four from one Killick over. Of course, he was helped by two no-balls. As far as I recall it was 4, 6, 6, 0,

4, 4, 4, 6. It stood as the world record till Garry Sobers hit 36 off Malcolm Nash in 1968. The record stayed with Nottinghamshire, though. Alletson saved the match.

AM: What I find most intriguing is that John Arlott wrote an entire book about the innings. Of course, it was an innings worth writing about. But then, how many books have been written about one innings?

AS: There have been books about a solitary match. The 1926 Test at The Oval, for example, has been written about by John Marchant. Ross wrote this one out here about that great Test match at Lord's in 1963, when Colin Cowdrey came in with his arm in plaster. Even *One More Run*, this Bomber Wells book by Stephen Chalke, is about one particular match. Recently John Lazenby wrote *Edging Towards Darkness* about the famous timeless Test at Durban, 1938/39, when Wally Hammond's Englishmen had to call off the match because they had to catch a boat.

AM: No, I'm talking about incidents in a match, a particular event in a match. *Alletson's Innings* is a rare example. There's Verity's 10-10 – a book was made out of it by Chris Waters.

AS: And that over from Nash to Sobers resulted in two books by Grahame Lloyd. *Six of the Best* and *Howzat? The Six Sixes Ball Mystery* were both quite nicely crafted – the second one less about the over and more about the ball that Sobers had belted around that day.

Curiously, all these books are about incidents in first-class cricket. Brian Scovell named his book on Laker *19 for 90*, but it was a biography of the great man. *W.G. Grace at Kadina* was all about the controversy surrounding W.G.'s side taking on Yorke's Peninsula at the Peninsular Oval during the 1873/74 tour.

You're right, there are very few books about one innings or one spell of bowling. The only other book with a similar theme that comes to mind is John Riley's account of the Alan Kippax–Hal Hooker partnership, very prosaically titled *10th wicket first class cricket record partnership: 307 runs: A.F. Kippax and J.E.H. Hooker, New South Wales, December 25th and 26th 1928*. Australian publication, so you have to sell a kidney to get it shipped to Europe.

AM: Or to India. There have been books written on complete Test matches. The 1926 Oval and the 1963 Lord's Test matches as you mentioned. The Brisbane tie of 1960/61 was the subject of at least one and a half books (Fingleton's *The Greatest Test of All*, Benaud's *A Tale of Two Tests*). Similarly, the Old Trafford Test match of 1961 got half of Benaud's book.

As for partnerships, Stephen Chalke did write *Five Five Five* on Sutcliffe and Holmes's stand worth the same number – though the 555th run was due to a scorer's post-facto intervention.

This may not be relevant, but the famous cigarette brand was *not* named after the partnership. In fact, the cigarette was made available for Sutcliffe and Holmes in the Yorkshire dressing room shortly after they reached that mark.

AS: Speaking of which, I do feel there are plenty of books that have not yet been written. If Alletson's innings deserves a volume – and I am not disputing that it does – there are so many feats in cricket that do deserve to be subjects of individual books.

Cricket is a unique game in that way. Amidst the greater story of a cricket match, there are often such phases of play, one-on-one battles, extraordinary sessions ... all of which are like great thrilling short stories packed into a greater novel. Sometimes the novel is great, sometimes it may be lousy – a drab, one-sided Test match for instance. But, the stories within always tend to be interesting. Take the Michael Holding spell to Brian Close and John Edrich at Old Trafford, 1976. Or even his over to Geoff Boycott at Barbados five years later.

AM: Or, perhaps, Eddie Gilbert's over to Bradman. Those five minutes, or thereabouts, would not only leave an impression on Bradman (he would remember it as the fastest bowling he had faced), it almost certainly helped the English team management become more assured about their strategy in the following season. At the same time, the over inspires the reader to dig deeper into the life of Gilbert, and ponder about the 'what if' – the prospect of a Gilbert versus Larwood duel in the Bodyline series.

AS: Daniel J. Boorstin wrote a book titled *Cleopatra's Nose*. Throw in Malcolm Marshall as a rather nasty character and we can do the same thing with Mike Gatting and his sniffer. Or if we go way back in time, the Jessop innings at The Oval, 1902. One of the most incredible feats of counterattack in the history of the game. A beautiful backdrop as well, with P.G. Wodehouse having to leave the ground just as the Jessop–Jackson partnership was taking shape, because his hour's break from his duties at the Hongkong and Shanghai Bank was over. I can see delightful chapters ready to be penned.

The Bradman feats of 309 in a day at Leeds and the 270 at Melbourne could also do with books, perhaps even epics in verse.

AM: The Chennai Test of 1998/99 between India and Pakistan also deserves a stirring book, with the drama of the final day matching the diplomatic intrigue of the resumption of Test cricket between the two countries after so many years.

Or the fifth day of the Ranji Trophy Final of 1990/91. Or Javed Miandad's last-ball six off Chetan Sharma. Or the second day's play at Ellis Park, 1953, when Bert Sutcliffe came back to bat after being hit on the head and Bob Blair joined him at the wicket, still mourning the death of his fiancée. Or the May-and-Cowdrey partnership in 1957.

AS: Of course, when I look back at all my years of cricket watching, I come up with my own favourites. I was there at Eden Gardens for every ball of the 2001 Test match. VVS Laxman's 281 in itself is a topic for epics. Then there was Anil Kumble bowling in West Indies with a bandaged jaw.

However, if I have to pick one phase of play that defied every accepted norm and logic of cricket in its sheer audacious brilliance, I'd go for the three hours at Newlands, Cape Town, 4 January 1997. There under Table Mountain, Tendulkar and Azharuddin laid out an exhibition fit for the cricketing gods.

AM: That three-hour session did little more than help India avoid the follow-on (and perhaps an innings defeat). It did not really have the opportunity to become a Laxman 281 or a Dravid 270 or a Gavaskar 221 or Vengsarkar 102 or a Viswanath 97, instances on which the matches could be won or drawn.

This was a backs-against-the-wall counterattack that most realised would be futile even before it had started. Back in the 1990s, despite their side's aura of invincibility at home, Indian cricket fans had got used to their heroes collapsing against pace in overseas conditions. And after scores of 100 and 66 at Durban, there was little expectation.

AS: It was a tale of some extraordinary batting to produce a glimmer of hope from what had seemed the darkest recess of desperation. A team of more experienced batsmen and a slightly better bowling attack could perhaps have made a match out of it after the miracle. But, that was the tale of touring Indian sides in the 1990s.

AM: Brilliant batting or brilliant bowling, any brilliant individual performance, cannot win matches by themselves. It is a complex game with 22 performances affecting the outcome. They can increase the probability of winning or saving a match. Cricket is that sort of a game.

AS: In terms of increasing the probability of saving the game, the partnership had done a superhuman job of lifting it from the negligible into the realms of significantly achievable.

AM: And it did so by counterattacking from both ends against a magnificent bowling attack from the most hopeless of positions.

AS: The sad part is that this particular Test match came at a curious period for cricket reportage. The recent explosion of satellite television had ensured that the images were beamed back live. So, people witnessed the miracle in real time. But the news channels specialising in creating sound and fury around events (and non-events) and repeating them till they are ingrained in the national DNA had not yet sprouted like mushrooms as they would in a few years.

AM: Till the first half of the 1990s, all the Indian viewers got to watch of Test matches from overseas were highlights packages, which consisted of little more than dismissals and boundaries. Now, with live telecast (and recordings) of away Test matches, one could also spot the vulnerabilities of their heroes, as they had done on this particular tour, what with Donald & co. steamrolling the Indians at Kingsmead.

AS: The internet was there, but 1995 to 1998 was part of what has become an online black hole. Archives end before that and new media starts afterwards. Cricinfo was in its infancy, and hence online reports did not spread around the web in the manner they would do within a few seasons.

So people saw the innings, marvelled, but not much was written about it. While journalists did cover the tour, a lot of contemporary reports we find are sketchy, brief to the point of telegram-speak, definitely not enough to contribute to a book like the one on Alletson's innings.

Strange, considering that if we scroll down a few years we can find an enormous amount of repetitive stuff written about far more mundane bits of cricket.

AM: It is a bit disappointing, because that one-year period after the 1996 World Cup was a defining one for Indian cricket. Azhar was removed from the captaincy after a six-year stint. He was replaced by Tendulkar. Every now and then the media houses had a field day at the slightest hint – often imaginary – of a cold war between the two. To be honest, the relationship between the two of them was not the warmest at that juncture.

Amidst all this, India found three young talents who would battle each other (though certainly not Tendulkar or Azhar) for slots in the middle order.

The struggles and success stories of all five were telecast live back home. The fans no longer had to wait for the morning's newspaper. This was when cricket journalism began to change, because there was little point in reliving a day's cricket, in conventional fashion, after everyone had watched the proceedings ball-by-ball.

Readers expected, and demanded, more. The spread of the internet in the 2000s and the rising importance of social media in the 2010s would change it further.

One must remember that before their 1996 tours of England and South Africa, India had toured only New Zealand since Kapil Dev's retirement. By now, the stars of the 1980s – Gavaskar, Kapil, Vengsarkar, Shastri – were all gone. The future looked uncertain for Manjrekar and Sidhu. Azhar and Tendulkar, the two involved in the partnership, were the only missing links between the era of grainy Doordarshan coverage and the satellite-powered telecast of incomparably superior quality.

AS: Yes, but this tour sort of slipped through the handover and, as I was saying, very sketchy details remain of the same. Somehow this partnership was hard done by the circumstances.

Often deeds in the game are remembered, eulogised and made immortal, because of the associated noise made by the contemporary commentators. Other equally brilliant deeds suffer by not being blessed with similar coverage.

For example, Vinoo Mankad captured 5-196 and scored 70 and 184 at Lord's in 1952. The circumstances were also special. He had been playing for Haslingden and had been recruited following an emergency call only after India had been destroyed at Headingley. Also, he played at Lord's, and anything done at Lord's becomes big news.

Ten years later Polly Umrigar scored 56 and 172 not out and captured 5-107 at Port-of-Spain. A feat of similar, if not greater, brilliance. But it was a match between India and West Indies in West Indies. The men who specialised in providing cricketing deeds with a permanent sheen of rhetoric were mostly English journalists and commentators.

Hence, Umrigar's feat is not really celebrated to that extent. To use a cliché, it has remained 'unsung'.

AM: In that small phase of time between 1995 and 1998, apart from the Tendulkar–Azharuddin partnership, there were three major batting performances in South Africa. Mark Waugh's 116 in Port Elizabeth that same season, Azhar Mahmood's 132 at Durban in 1997/98 and Mike Atherton's 185 not out at Johannesburg in 1995/96. Of all these, only the Atherton innings keeps getting recalled. The others have been neglected.

AS: This is perhaps because the English press composed odes about it at that time and have not really stopped revisiting it. The same was not really true with the others.

AM: There are numerous other examples of this. For example, 2019 witnessed two of the greatest Test innings of all time, from Kusal Perera and Ben Stokes. Of the many arguments raised by those – experts included – in favour of Stokes's performance is that his innings came in the Ashes.

AS: The two innings were comparable, but there was no competition between the respective sound bites.

AM: Similarly, the West Indian fast bowlers' spell against India at Sabina Park in 1975/76 is much less talked about – at a global level, that is, among Indian fans it's a different matter – than that one afternoon of Roberts and Holding steaming in at Close and Edrich. There is little doubt that the first caused significantly more physical damage.

AS: Tony Greig's 'grovel' comment and the stark opportunities of painting the scene in black and white did play their roles. It depends on the moment in history as well.

Victor Trumper's heroics and exciting batting style moved many an English writer to eulogies that poured forth at the very moment that the newly federated nation of Australia was looking for heroes. When we look at it with statistically aware eyes from the distance of a century and more, we do find that over the same career-span Clem Hill's efforts were perhaps superior, especially against more demanding foes. But, the Trumper tales live on till today, riding on the euphoria of the turn of the last century. Even now books continue to be written about him. Hill is mainly remembered for punching Peter McAllister (although the punch was perhaps as worthy a blow for Australian cricket and cricketers).

Coming back to this particular partnership between Tendulkar and Azhar, the lack of reportage is really quite disappointing – because the intricate historical connections of the two nations, the complex economic situation and the glorious geographical backdrop, alongside the sheer brilliance of batting … with the added garnishing of the visit of Nelson Mandela on that very day … these together produce a tale with drama written all over it. It is a story waiting to be told. A book waiting to be written.

AM: So why don't *we* write it? We have the material, we have watched it live, we have followed cricket in both countries thereafter through their highs and lows …

And thus we decided … on the spur of the moment … to fill this gap in the annals of cricket literature as well as in fan memories with the drama, the brilliance and the complicated mesh of historical backdrop, future dynamics between the two countries and their respective cricket boards.

Evening

By the time Paul Adams completes his curiously convoluted frog-in-the-blender follow-through, the ball has already pitched on the middle stump. The googly turns past a clueless blade and crashes into the stumps. Adams does his characteristic celebratory flip, the head ducking, the body contorted into a ball, the feet flying through the air before landing on the other side, every such celebration sending palpitations through the South African team management, selectors and physios.

Who on earth sends in Venkatesh Prasad as a nightwatchman anyway? An average of 4.87 from eight Tests. Why not the far more capable Anil Kumble or Javagal Srinath?

On the other hand, it has been a curiously intelligent move by Hansie Cronje. With his batsmen, primarily Lance Klusener, creaming the Indian bowlers, he and Bob Woolmer probably had a lot of time to work things out. Batting at the fag-end of the day, with that tottering top order, a nightwatchman was always on the cards. Perhaps they had a plan for each one of them. Unfortunately, we can no longer ask them. But that is a different story.

Prasad could probably have missed a few from the faster men and survived, too poor a batsman to get a touch to Allan Donald and Shaun Pollock. Adams was the right choice. A wrist-spinner with a splendid wrong 'un. Prasad has to either play him with his bat or go. He goes.

Captain Sachin Tendulkar is not very pleased to walk in with minutes remaining in the day. With 3,106 runs in 46 Tests, he is a few years into his decade-and-a-half-long tussle for the crown of world batsmanship with Brian Lara. Impeccable consistency laced with audacious improvisations on the platform of perfect technique on one side, a genius on a coil of spring with a penchant for mammoth knocks on the other. A rivalry to be savoured.

But introduction to captaincy has not been easy for the Indian master's willow. For the first time in three years, his career average has dipped just under 50. In five Tests as captain he averages 19.50, with just one half-century. With moments to go, this is the worst time to come out and take guard.

Sourav Ganguly greets him with a nervous nod of his head. He has struck a couple of boundaries. In fact, his has been the only blade from which runs have looked like coming in this innings.

Rahul Dravid was dropped on 1, and chopped one from Lance Klusener on to his stumps for 2. The end to 55 minutes and 41 balls of painful, pitiable struggle.

W.V. Raman went way earlier, his perennially lazy saunter across the pitch for a second run failing to beat the fierce Protean agility. It was Klusener with the throw. Eight wickets in the second innings on debut at Eden Gardens. Now 102 not out in 100 deliveries in his fourth Test, followed by a run-out and a wicket. Test cricket seems easy for some.

Tendulkar takes guard.

AS: I remember sitting in the lounge of the hostel of my university, watching the game. I could feel my fingers tightening around the handle of the mug of tea. A fairly large number had suddenly gathered in front of the television in the last few minutes, some curious chain of whispers informing everyone that Tendulkar was at the wicket. Mind you, this was long before the explosion of text messages. The hearts seemed to thud with every step the bowler took after turning from his bowling mark, and by the time the little man went forward to meet the ball mine was knocking against my front teeth. That was what the wicket of Tendulkar meant in those days.

AM: It was not an exaggeration, you know, what they say about television sets being switched off when he got out. I used to watch every ball, even when India needed 170 with two wickets standing, but many others used to switch their sets off as soon as Tendulkar was dismissed. It was eerie. There used to be a collective groan across the neighbourhood, and then the boys came out to play their own cricket. Mind you, Azhar might still have been batting, but none of that mattered.

Tendulkar's stature among a section of cricket followers was already godlike, enough to generate discomfort even among many of his fans. Indian batsmen of the new millennium would go on to achieve many a feat, as individuals or as a unit, but the 'god' tag would stay.

It was an honour or a burden – depending on your point of view – that he still has to bear.

AS: I remember watching the previous overseas series. In England. The Edgbaston Test match. We were sitting in the television room of our hostel in New Delhi. It was teeming with people as Tendulkar played that 122-run gem. The next highest score in the innings was 18. As long as he was there, people dared to hope.

That was the difference. Since the early 1990s the limits of possibility had been redrawn. The logical parameters of match situation had been tampered with. Every opposition captain had to take the Tendulkar factor into consideration. As long as he was there, genuine impossibilities looked within reach.

I still recall him skying a pull off Chris Lewis. By the time the catch was taken, the TV room had emptied. Only two or three still lingered.

AM: Unfortunately, that hundred, the best from either side in the series, is not remembered as much as some subsequent ones. That said, Ganguly and Dravid started their careers on that tour, and then Laxman, and later Sehwag came into the team. This would ensure that the TV sets were not switched off to that degree the moment Tendulkar got out.

Why was Tendulkar such a demigod?

India, with its closed economy, license-raj and slow, hesitant stumble across the path of progress, was one of the last to embrace the idiot box. Even considering the other third-world countries, India was a late entrant.

To put this in context, people in Pakistan had already been watching television programmes for more than a decade before the first set appeared in a common Indian home.

(Under the apartheid regime, South Africa had to wait longer. It was not until 1976 that the first sets appeared in the country.)

In the 1980s, international matches at home became regular fare on Indian television, and slowly one-day internationals played overseas were also watched live. But when the side went on Test tours to countries other than Pakistan, the fans had to depend on packaged highlights.

In 1991, under pressure from the World Bank and IMF, India was forced to open its economy and allow foreign investment. The market, which had remained closed and constrained, opened up and along with that cable television made an entrance.

Soon cable operators were running amok and elders in middle-class housing colonies were gravely shaking their grey heads, wondering about the onset of decadence that the distractions of 24-hour television would inflict on the future generations. But their feeble resistance did not quite prosper. Even the Gulf War could now be followed on television, after all. Urban India was soon enmeshed with cables. First the cities, and then gradually the small towns and villages fell to this invasion.

The year 1991 also saw another major change. With India hosting the path-breaking ODI tour of the recently back-in-the-fold South Africa, two television channels of the Rainbow Nation contacted the BCCI for television rights. It was a jolt for the board who till now had often paid Doordarshan for telecasting the home Tests and ODIs. No one quite knew who owned the rights. After much leafing through the fine print, it was discovered that the BCCI were indeed the owners. It made the board realise that they had been unwittingly sitting on an untapped goldmine.

It took a certain amount of gestation period for this potential money-spinner to reach its logical conclusion and coffers. ESPN and TWI (Trans World International) started transforming the way Indians viewed home

Test matches, but the foreign tours remained mainly relegated to ODIs and packaged highlights.

The New Zealand tour of 1993/94 was the first to have the solitary Test match beamed back live, but it was a relatively low-key affair. All that changed in 1996.

It was Mark Mascarenhas, the Connecticut-based businessman of Indian origin later to become Tendulkar's agent, who performed the magical transformation of cricket viewership in India. He zeroed in on the 1996 World Cup played in the subcontinent and showed the BCCI the enormous market that lay in selling television rights. He bought the rights for an atrocious sum, and the profits he made were equally spectacular. The transmissions reached the remotest parts of India, and also the cricket-starved diasporas around the world, mainly in the United States. The world woke up to the power of televising cricket in India and to Indians around the world. Indian cricket lovers in the remotest villages and the farthest diasporas started watching every ball that was bowled.

By then the Indian television industry had come of age. From the one television channel (two in Delhi) when Tendulkar had made his debut in 1989, there were over 50 by 1996.

The 1996 World Cup witnessed major commercialisation. Ex-cricketers recruited as commentators were star attractions themselves. Every possible and impossible product was packaged with cricketing essence during the tournament, from the official soft drink to the official chewing gum. Advertisements were beamed to the remote towns, featuring men of the stature of Courtney Walsh and Dickie Bird.

Now to gauge the appeal of Sachin Tendulkar, let us look at what transpired in the transitional five years following the satellite television revolution of cricket, the revolution that was kick-started with the 1996 World Cup.

From February 1996 to the end of the 2000/01 season, Sachin Tendulkar led the rest of the field by light years. No Indian batsman had reached the top of the batting charts by dominating the best bowlers in this way, being so far ahead of the rest of the field across the world. And the television channels beamed each and every stroke, taking them to every cricket-loving home in India and around the world.

Be it the desert storms at Sharjah, or the Test hundreds at Birmingham '96, Cape Town '97, Chennai '98, Chennai '99 or Melbourne '99, the story was always of genius unfolding.

To put the difference between Tendulkar and the rest of the batsmen in this period in perspective, it makes sense to look at some data. Both the figures in the Test matches and ODIs indicate Tendulkar was playing on a level of his own.

Generally, combining different formats together does not make sense in gauging the quality of a batsman. The units are totally different. However, if we consider the viewers who watched cricket on television in those days and cheered runs and hundreds irrespective of the format, during those five years between World Cup 1996 and the Australian tour of India in 2001, Tendulkar scored 11,204 runs in international cricket with 41 centuries! No one came anywhere close.

With television converting international cricket to prime-time entertainment, people sat back during those initial years and discovered their superhero who zoomed through the cricketing stratosphere while the lesser mortals had to make their way across the ground.

The statistics were such that they even cut right through the oft-used inane cricketing argument for safeguarding the interests of one's own heroes – numbers-don't-give-the-complete-picture-because-I-would-rather-believe-something-else.

World Cup 1996 to 2000/01 season (Tests)

Batsman	T	R	Ave	100	50
Sachin Tendulkar	44	4,237	60.52	17	13
Steve Waugh	54	3,963	51.46	14	14
Alec Stewart	55	3,681	40.45	7	20
Rahul Dravid	43	3,660	53.82	9	18
Gary Kirsten	53	3,541	41.17	11	14
Brian Lara	49	3,485	40.05	8	17
Daryll Cullinan	51	3,459	46.74	13	11
Mark Waugh	57	3,454	39.25	8	20
Michael Atherton	52	3,207	35.63	7	16
Nasser Hussain	52	3,010	35.83	9	13

World Cup 1996 to 2000/01 season (ODIs)

Batsman	M	R	Ave	SR	100	50
Sachin Tendulkar	166	6,967	46.13	89.25	24	29
Sourav Ganguly	162	6,374	44.57	73.69	16	36
Saeed Anwar	141	5,546	43.32	83.94	11	32
Mark Waugh	126	5,001	44.65	76.09	13	27
Sanath Jayasuriya	136	4,825	37.40	97.21	10	33
Inzamam-ul-Haq	147	4,620	39.82	70.48	3	35
Rahul Dravid	144	4,596	36.76	67.91	7	30
Michael Bevan	134	4,461	54.40	75.31	5	31
Gary Kirsten	114	4,406	42.77	73.65	8	30
Ajay Jadeja	154	4,189	38.78	73.84	5	23
Ijaz Ahmed	129	4,173	36.92	79.91	6	27
Andy Flower	133	4,147	34.27	74.25	1	36
Marvan Atapattu	119	4,049	38.93	65.78	5	32

AM: India being a batting-crazy nation, it was mostly the Indian batsmen the brands targeted. Ganguly, Dravid and later Sehwag all became huge brand names.

AS: Sports superstars becoming brands has been a feature for a long time now. From Michael Jordan to David Beckham to Tiger Woods to Cristiano Ronaldo to Roger Federer, all of them are supreme brands.

In India towards the end of the 1990s it was helped further by the proliferation of television channels, riding on advertisements and cricket-crazed sound bites.

India never quite managed to produce too many world-class bowlers until the very recent years as we write. Unlike Pakistan, for instance, with their steady supply of fast-bowling greats. Hence, to keep hanging on to the national craze surrounding cricket, there is a fascination for batsmen and near mythical powers attributed to them. The brands obviously built on this.

Brand wars

A lot of brands had already zeroed in on Tendulkar before the 1996 boom.

This was a ready-made superhero, whose performances, as we have seen, branded him as such.

When other brand ambassadors were identified and backed in those years, it was difficult to replicate Tendulkar-like performances on the 22 yards. That is evident from the data.

Hence, different branding strategies were used for some cricketers, creating brand essence, seldom concrete, often spurious. Superpowers not directly mappable to performance, not always dealing with deeds with bat and ball, had to be created and bestowed.

Sometimes they don't stand up to careful data analysis unless considerably stretched.

AM: The sad thing is that in spite of this fascination with batsmen, there was not much Indian batting on display at Durban.

AS: 100 and 66 at Durban. Team scores, not individual. On one of the fastest possible surfaces. There was a surge of hope when Prasad took a fifer and South Africa were bowled out for 235 on the first day. The euphoria lasted only until the match restarted on the morrow. 100 all out in just 39.1 overs. That was not the worst of it. Five more to Prasad in the second innings. A total of 259. The target 395. No one expected India to overhaul it. But no one really expected them to be knocked over for 66.

AM: I was talking to G. Viswanath, who had covered the tour for *The Hindu*. A local journalist had told him that India were fortunate to get even 100 and 66. In his opinion India would have scored even less, had the clouds been lower that day.

The Prasad spell was another matter. Prasad took 10-153 in the Test match. The South Africans got 10-100 in India's first innings. Srinath took five wickets. Had there been a third world-class seamer, the way India have now, things might have been different – to some extent.

Even here in Cape Town, Srinath captured 3-130 and Prasad 3-114, but the others had 0-285 (Kirsten was run out and South Africa declared with seven wickets down). That was the kind of difference the lack of that extra fast bowler made. India might have been up against 329, not 529, had there been a bit of support for the two of them.

Srinath, Prasad, and South Africa

The result of the series could have been different, had India had a third seamer to share the workload when they needed a break.

Donald was the outstanding bowler of the series, but between them, Srinath and Prasad took a comparable number of wickets (they took more wickets than the Donald–Pollock pair), and had to bowl more overs.

Both pairs bore half the workload for their respective sides. But while the other South African bowlers claimed 43% of their team's wickets, their Indian counterparts contributed with only 29%.

All bowlers on India's tour of South Africa, 1996/97

Player	B	W	Ave	Player	B	W	Ave
Srinath	889	18	28.72	Donald	716	20	15.95
Prasad	732	17	25.00	Pollock	576	10	23.10
Combined	1,621	35	26.91	Combined	1,292	30	18.33
Others	1,667	14	57.57	Others	1,501	23	32.96
	49%	71%	(*)		46%	57%	(*)

*The percentage figures denote the percentage of balls bowled and wickets taken by the Srinath–Prasad and Donald–Pollock duos respectively.

Prasad's 10-153 at Kingsmead remains the best analysis by an Indian seamer against South Africa, home or away. Sreesanth's 8-99 in 2005/06 is a somewhat distant second, followed by Srinath's 8-104 in 2001/02.

EVENING

As for Srinath, only four pace bowlers have taken more wickets than his 64 at 24.48 against South Africa in the post-war era. Of them, only Statham (69 wickets at 20.67) has a better average.

Perhaps it is not relevant in the context of the book, but do take a look at the figures of Sydney Barnes. A whopping 83 wickets, an average below 10, and 12 five-wicket hauls. In fact, he took ten wickets in six of the seven Tests he played against them. Could have been another ...

Fast bowlers against South Africa (50 wickets)

Player	M	W	Ave	5WI	10WM
James Anderson	26	93	31.53	4	-
Sydney Barnes	7	83	9.85	12	6
Stuart Broad	22	75	30.12	2	-
Brian Statham	16	69	20.67	4	1
Mitchell Johnson	12	64	25.64	3	2
Javagal Srinath	**13**	**64**	**24.48**	**4**	**0**
Glenn McGrath	17	57	27.33	2	0
Chris Martin	14	55	26.73	4	1
Alec Bedser	13	54	26.98	3	1
Courtney Walsh	10	51	19.80	2	0
Brett Lee	14	50	34.64	2	0

AS: When Donald and Pollock took breaks, South Africa had Klusener and McMillan running in for them. And then there was Cronje with his brand of medium pace. By the way, Klusener and McMillan both scored hundreds in this Test match. In the first innings Klusener and McMillan added an unbeaten 147. In the second innings McMillan and Pollock added an unbeaten 101.

AM: Yes, that was the other difference between the sides. Other than Donald, all the South African pacemen were genuine all-rounders, in stark contrast to their Indian counterparts. The scales were tipped too heavily in favour of the hosts.

AS: There have always been all-rounders in South African cricket, starting with Jimmy Sinclair at the turn of the last century.

Of the great googly bowling quartet, Aubrey Faulkner was perhaps the greatest all-rounder in the history of the game alongside Garry Sobers, Keith Miller and Imran Khan. Reggie Schwarz and Bertie Vogler could both bat. And Gordon White was a classy batsman, who turned his arm over to bowl googlies now and then. Besides, Tip Snooke, Dave Nourse ... most of them were all-rounders. Even the first non-white South African Test cricketer, Charlie 'Buck' Llewellyn.

AM: The 1960s team had Eddie Barlow, Mike Procter, and even Peter Pollock and Tiger Lance. And, of course, Basil D'Oliveira. Then there was Clive Rice in the apartheid era and of course Tony Greig who went to play for England.

AS: Adrian Kuiper as well. And through much of the 1950s and 1960s the pillar at the top of the order and the regular third pacer was Trevor Goddard, one of the most underrated all-round greats in history. There was Clive van Ryneveld as well, who, apart from batting and bowling, fielded superbly at short-leg, led the South African cricket team and was a rugby international for England during his Oxford days.

If we look at the non-white cricketers who played during the apartheid days, there was Taliep Salie – a leg-spinning all-rounder. Clarrie Grimmett, who saw him on the 1935/36 tour, voiced that Salie would get into any side in the world. In 2000, Gesant Toffar noted in his obituary that he had been a better all-round cricketer than D'Oliveira. Not that non-empirical comparisons are too trustworthy, but it underlines what a fantastic player he was.

Then there were Cec Abrahams, the Abed brothers Goolam and 'Tiny' … fantastic all-rounders who played in the South African non-European side against the Kenyan Asians and the East Africans in the second half of the 1950s. 'Tiny' Abed was reputed to be an attacking batsman and a dangerous swing bowler in the mould of Keith Miller.

AM: And once they returned, they almost immediately had McMillan, followed by Pollock, Klusener and, finally, Kallis. There were excellent limited-overs all-rounders like Cronje, Boje, and in later days, Albie Morkel.

AS: Even Pat Symcox, who played as an off-spinner and batted mostly at No. 9, scored a Test hundred from No. 10 and a fifty from No. 11, ending with a batting average of 28.50. And later they had Vernon Philander.

In 2013, during an interview with the late Clive Rice I asked why there were so many all-rounders in South Africa. His answer was quite simplistic. 'If you're in the nets to practise and you do both bowling and batting properly, you are contributing. In the match you're always in the game. If you get out for a duck, you don't spend your time standing at third man. You can pick up five wickets and it is great again. This appealed to me. I guess it appealed to all those guys.'

South African all-rounders in Test cricket

Name	M	R	Ave	100	W	Ave	5WI
Jimmy Sinclair	25	1,069	23.23	3	63	31.68	1
Buck Llewellyn	15	544	20.14	0	48	29.60	4
Dave Nourse	45	2,234	29.78	1	41	37.87	0
Aubrey Faulkner	25	1,754	40.79	4	82	26.58	4

Name	M	R	Ave	100	W	Ave	5WI
Cyril Vincent	25	526	20.23	0	84	31.32	3
Trevor Goddard	41	2,516	34.46	1	123	26.22	5
Eddie Barlow	30	2,516	45.74	6	40	34.05	1
Peter Pollock	28	607	21.67	0	116	24.18	9
Mike Procter	4	226	25.11	0	41	15.02	1
Hansie Cronje	68	3,714	36.41	6	43	29.95	0
Brian McMillan	38	1,968	39.36	3	75	33.82	0
Shaun Pollock	108	3,781	32.31	2	421	23.11	16
Jacques Kallis	165	13,206	55.25	45	291	32.63	5
Lance Klusener	49	1,906	32.86	4	80	37.91	1
Vernon Philander	64	1,779	24.04	0	224	22.32	13

South African all-rounders in rebel 'Tests'

Name	M	R	Ave	100	W	Ave	5WI
Adrian Kuiper	7	216	24.00	0	16	19.18	1
Clive Rice	18	679	27.16	0	28	22.39	0
Brian McMillan	4	111	22.20	0	10	31.20	0
Alan Kourie	16	407	23.94	0	38	33.60	3

The South African all-rounders were brilliant in the non-Test world as well, but often away from international eyes. These two, in particular, were glittering stars of county cricket:

Legendary all-rounders in first-class cricket

Name	M	R	Ave	100	W	Ave	5WI
Mike Procter	401	21,936	36.01	48	1,417	19.53	70
Clive Rice	482	26,331	40.95	48	930	22.49	23

And unfortunately, some had to perform away from all eyes but those of their own people.

The non-white all-rounders the world did not get to know about

Taliep Salie: Leg-spinner par excellence and a good batsman to boot. Some said he was a greater all-round cricketer than even Basil D'Oliveira.

Cec Abrahams: Fast-medium bowler of considerable ability and a very dependable batsman.

'Tiny' Abed: Fast-bowling all-rounder in the Keith Miller mould. At 6ft 3in he was called Tiny because brother Lobo, a superb wicketkeeper, was two inches taller.

Goolam Abed: Off-spinning all-rounder, another fabulously talented cricketer from the Abed family.

Denis Foreman: Managed to slip through the colour bar and play three matches for Western Province in the Currie Cup of 1951/52. Migrated to England where his football skills earned him a contract with Brighton and Hove Albion. From 1952 to 1967, he played 125 first-class matches for Sussex.

Eric Majola: Splendid Eastern Province all-rounder who was also a top-class rugby fly-half.

Khaya Majola: In the inter-provincial matches for non-whites between 1971 and 1991, Khaya Majola scored 2,735 runs (second highest), captured 214 wickets with his left-arm spin (fifth highest) and took 65 catches (highest).

Tendulkar and Ganguly survive the rest of the day, but the scoreboard says it all. 29/3 in response to 529/7. Not really fascinating reading for the Indian fans. The age-old tale of abject surrender abroad.

And since the England tour, the overseas woes were being beamed back live.

The mood in the dressing room is anything but upbeat. And around the world the Indian fans gingerly lick their wounds.

Cape Town

The sun sets over Table Mountain. This is Cape Town. The first port of call of the Europeans. The Dutch settled here in 1652, the British took over in 1806.

After that it remained a subcontinent of prolonged tussle. A tussle between British imperialism and capitalism, and the nomadic farming ways of the descendants of the Dutch, who became the orthodox Bible-abiding Afrikaners.

They fought for control over the land, more so when diamond and gold were discovered. The land was split into four colonies, two English and two Dutch. It all came to a head in the prolonged 1899–1902 conflict, the Boer War.

There were, of course, other wars. Wars not given that prominence in the chronicles penned down over the years. Wars through which the indigenous African tribes were driven off the lands that had been theirs for centuries. They were called the Frontier Wars.

After the Boer War peace was brokered between the two warring white factions, and soon South Africa became a union. Before and after that the chips of negotiation between the British and the Boers were the black, coloured and Indian communities. To cater for both the two white races, the non-whites were increasingly marginalised.

By 1913, the blacks, who formed 80% of the population, were restricted to 7% of the country in their settlements.

And things turned from terrible to diabolical when the National Party won the 1948 elections and apartheid became the government policy.

Basil D'Oliveira

It was in this very Cape Town, near Table Mountain, that Basil D'Oliveira grew up as an enormously talented Cape-Coloured cricketer.

The term meant that he was mixed race. In his own words: 'I am not certain of the sociology of our past, and when asked what is a Cape-Coloured, I can only repeat what we grew up to understand it to be. A Cape-Coloured is someone not Indian, not African, but a combination of either Indian and white or African and white. Out of this mixing a new race was born. In South Africa, if you are mixed you are coloured, and that's the end of it.'

Being coloured, he perhaps had it slightly better than the blacks and the Indians. At least as far as the basic rights and amenities were concerned, and at least until 1948. But there could be no hope, no dream of playing international cricket for South Africa.

A phenomenal talent, in his twenties D'Oliveira played in the non-white tournaments – the David Harris Trophy for the coloured, the Dadabhay Trophy contested between the non-white races. And then he led the non-white South Africans in a couple of triumphant series against the Kenyan Asians and the East Africans.

But international cricket remained a dream against the terrible apartheid legislations. When he watched Test matches at this very Newlands Ground, it was from the Cage, the segregated enclosure for the non-Europeans.

Morning

On the third morning Tendulkar bats against throwdowns. He tries shuffling back and across to a few. It feels good. The timing is pleasing. He decides to try the approach when he resumes his innings.

AS: This was the second visit of an Indian cricket team to South Africa. They had played each other regularly since South Africa's re-admission, and continue to do so. Rice and his men visited in 1991, the first international cricket played by a South African side since re-admission. Azhar and his men returned the visit in 1992/93. This particular series was part of a back-to-back affair – the 1996 winter in India, followed by the 1996/97 summer in South Africa.

AM: Indian cricket was going through transition. In the space of three months they had found three batsmen who would join Tendulkar to form the middle order in the next decade, but these were still early days in their careers.

However, while this was a somewhat shaky transformation, India were taking giant strides towards taking over as the dominant force in the ICC.

AS: There had been a massive change to the country's cricketing fortunes due to the 1996 World Cup. Satellite television, branding, sponsorship, exploding popularity of the game, the reach into every nook and corner of the huge population.

AM: That ascent began after N.K.P. Salve was denied tickets for the 1983 World Cup Final. A smarting Salve vowed to bring the World Cup to the subcontinent. With Reliance as sponsors, India and Pakistan muscled the World Cup out of England, and became the hosts in 1987. They hosted it again in 1996, with Sri Lanka joining forces.

The ascent of satellite TV in India

In the early 1990s two men – Jagmohan Dalmiya and I.S. Bindra – played key roles in bringing an end to the impossibly ridiculous arrangement of the BCCI paying the Indian government's Doordarshan TV network to cover matches played in India.

The BCCI had sold rights for England's 1992/93 tour of India – the first home series in over two and a half years – to Trans World International (TWI). Doordarshan had to pay TWI USD1,000,000 to televise the matches in India. The BCCI made a profit of USD600,000 in the process. The die had been cast.

Realising that they now had to dish out money to cover matches, Doordarshan offered INR10,000,000 ($320,000) to the Cricket Association of Bengal (CAB) to cover the Hero Cup in late 1993. Unfortunately for them, this was significantly less than the TWI offer (INR17,600,000 and 70% share of global revenue for the event).

But Doordarshan did not concede defeat. They refused to pay TWI for footage, thereby depriving Indians of free-to-air viewership of the event; they went back to their previous policy of charging to cover matches (INR500,000 a match, this time); and refused to share advertising revenue.

Two days before the tournament, the Information and Broadcasting Ministry cited the archaic 1885 Indian Telegraph Act and announced that Indian government agencies were the only ones authorised to 'telecast any event live by uplinking signals from Indian soil' – an issue that had not been raised when TWI had covered the England series.

The initial matches of the tournament served little purpose once Pakistan had pulled out. Ten league matches to eliminate Zimbabwe from a five-team pool generated little interest. When the tournament got underway with an India–Sri Lanka clash at Kanpur, the on-field advertising was minimal. CAB, already hit badly by Pakistan's decision, seemed to be headed for a massive revenue loss. The tournament picked up pace and excitement only towards the end.

The Indian government did not help, either. Riding the inertia of half a century of bureaucracy, the customs departments at Delhi, Bombay, and Calcutta airports seized TWI equipment on the grounds that relevant approval from government officials had not been obtained. These had to be recovered following an order from the Supreme Court.

The tussle sent ripples across the world. The South Africans never got to watch their match against Zimbabwe. Ali Bacher expressed concern regarding the telecast of the match against West Indies back home. Things escalated to such a degree that Nelson Mandela was soon making attempts to reach out to P.V. Narasimha Rao, then prime minister of India. The following year, Bacher threatened to withdraw South Africa's support for the subcontinent as host for the 1996 World Cup.

While the Hero Cup went ahead, conflicts over the right to telecast cricket in India were not resolved until February 1995, when Justices P.B. Sawant, B.P. Jeevan Reddy, and S. Mohan passed the following order:

'The airwaves or frequencies are public property. Their use has to be controlled and regulated by a public authority in the interests of the public and to prevent the invasion of their rights. The right to impart and receive information is a species of the right to freedom of speech and expression guaranteed by Article 19(1)(a) of the Constitution. A citizen has a fundamental right to use the best means of imparting and receiving information and as such to have access to telecasting for the purpose.'

Mark Mascarenhas had meanwhile gone ahead and signed a deal with Doordarshan. Once they got the all-clear, the relieved group of broadcasters went ahead and bought telecast rights from WorldTel for their respective territories.

However, the all-important out-of-court settlement with Doordarshan did not take place till a week ahead of the 1996 World Cup. Once that happened, satellite coverage of cricket became a permanent feature on television screens across India.

Twenty-two years after that World Cup, Star Sports bought IPL rights for five years from the BCCI for INR 163,475 million. ($2.55 billion)

AS: Along with India becoming a financial superpower in cricket, there were other reasons for the back-to-back tours. Cricket, as always, was linked to the diplomatic relations between the two nations.

The diplomatic pitch

In December 1996, Thabo Mbeki, deputy president of South Africa, was on a state visit to India. The same Thabo Mbeki who had once got drunk with the West Indian cricketers while celebrating a win during the 1966 summer, when Garry Sobers and his men were conquering England.

A number of agreements relating to culture, double taxation, fiscal evasion and a memorandum of understanding relating to defence equipment, were signed between the two countries.

On 28 March 1997, President Nelson Mandela and Prime Minister of India H.D. Deve Gowda would sign the Red Fort Declaration on a Strategic Partnership during Mandela's state visit to India.

AM: India and South Africa were linked through a long, long history. And cricketing relations reinforced the bonds.

AS: Yes, the ties between the two countries were always there, earlier than we generally deduce. In fact, cricketing relations actually did not start from 1991 as widely believed. They went back way earlier.

Relation between India and South Africa – cricketing and otherwise

The Indian population of South Africa was primarily centred in Natal, having been recruited as coolie labour from India during the 1860s.

During the course of the years, a large percentage became tradesmen and shop owners.

Indians often had the worst of the non-white lot during the era of segregation and legalised apartheid.

Curiously, they were not granted citizenship until 1961, having been variously labelled as an 'Asiatic curse' and a 'strange and foreign element that is not assimilable'.

Alongside the white criminals, these Asiatics were initially banned from entering Orange Free State. Later they were provided with passes valid for 24 hours to carry out goods deliveries. In the other parts of South Africa, they suffered from oppressive legislation.

In 1906, the Asian Registration Act was passed, requiring all Indians to register and carry passes.

In 1946, the Indian Representative Act was repealed, and the Asiatic Land Tenure Act essentially stopped Asians from owning or occupying new property without a permit. The act struck at the heart of Indian commercial and economic life, affecting trade and property matters, and making it virtually impossible for the Indian people to earn a decent living.

In fact, they did not face racial discrimination only from the ruling whites. In 1949, for example, there took place the Durban riots. It was targeted at the Indians in Durban and predominantly instigated by the Zulus, resulting in the deaths of 142 people and destruction of 58 shops and 247 dwellings.

During the segregation of the early 20th century and the apartheid era, the Indians in South Africa had their own thriving cricket scene.

In fact, the first South African cricket team to visit India was not Clive Rice's men of 1991.

Way back in November 1921, a team of football and cricket players comprising South African Indians from Durban had visited India on a two-month tour. They called themselves Christopher's Contingent after the chief organiser Albert Christopher, an influential advocate, war hero, and a former non-white tournament cricketer.

Sailing on board the *Kargola*, the touring party arrived in India in late November 1921 and played 14 games of football across Bombay, Banaras, Allahabad, Ahmedabad, Agra, Delhi, Madras, Calcutta and Poona, along with two games of cricket in Calcutta.

The visitors did not quite represent the cream of South African Indian cricket, partly because the focus was on football and partly because several of the best cricketers could not get four months' leave from their jobs.

Apart from playing two cricket matches in Calcutta, skipper Billy Subban and vice-captain Baboolal Maharaj were requested by the Mohun Bagan cricket side to turn out for them in a club game against Ballygunge.

This actually disproves another long-held view that the traditional Mohun Bagan club did not recruit any foreign player till the Nigerian footballer Chima Okorie played for them in 1991. Yes, Mohun Bagan had an almost Yorkshire-like obstinacy in this regard.

The South African Indian side also met Mahatma Gandhi at Ahmedabad and were assisted by the Indian Olympic Association in the organisation of the matches.

When they returned, there were serious attempts on the part of the organisers of South African Indian cricket to get the Natal Indian side into the Bombay Quadrangular on a regular basis. Unfortunately, that did not materialise.

The South African Indians formed their parallel cricket board, the South African Indian Cricket Union (SAICU), in 1940.

Later in the 1950s the non-white cricket bodies of the Africans, coloured and Indian communities created their combined South African Cricket Board of Control (SACBOC). United in this way, they started looking for international opportunities even as Test cricket was contested by the white South African team.

Using the Indian connections of SAICU, the administrators travelled to meet Indian board president Anthony de Mello, trying to arrange a visit of an Indian cricket side to play the non-white South African side. A non-white visiting team playing non-white South Africans was acceptable according to the colour-linked legislation of the apartheid regime.

However, the Indians were a Test-playing nation, and prioritised their commitment to the ICC. They did not respond favourably.

There was another tour that has all but fallen off the record books with time.

In 1934, the Indian Football Association XI crossed the Indian Ocean to play 19 matches in South Africa, most of them in Natal. They won 18 of the games, mostly by big margins, losing one solitary match.

The visitors showed exceptional skill in playing barefoot, but the white football bodies were not interested in taking them on.

AM: And of course, there is the Gandhi connection.

AS: Yes, the formative days of Gandhi were spent in that country, where over a period of 21 years he developed from an unknown young lawyer into the fully formed thorn in the British imperial flesh.

Gandhi in South Africa

It was in this Indian population of Natal that M.K. Gandhi, way before he became Mahatma, arrived in 1893 as an unknown 23-year-old law clerk. It was an effort to launch a legal career that had been stalled for more than a year.

His only mission on arrival had been to assist in a civil suit between two Muslim trading firms with roots in Porbandar. The skills he brought to the table were fluency in English and Gujarati, and recent legal training in London.

It is perhaps relevant to note here that when he had gone to London, Gandhi had carried a letter of introduction to another young man from his state who had recently arrived in England. This second Indian youth was called Kumar Shri Ranjitsinhji.

At Pietermaritzburg, Gandhi was ejected from a first-class compartment because a white passenger objected to having to share space with a 'coolie'.

The incident is seldom recounted in full. The young lawyer eventually got his way. The next morning, he fired telegrams to the general manager of the railway and his sponsor in Durban. He was finally allowed to reboard the same train from the same station the following night under the protection of the stationmaster and occupied a first-class berth.

Gandhi the activist was born.

His original intention had been to stay in the country for a year at the most. It ended in a 21-year sojourn. Gandhi left in July 1914. By then he was a seasoned 44-year-old politician, negotiator, leader of mass movement, author of a doctrine for struggles, a prolific political pamphleteer, and a self-taught evangelist on spiritual, nutritional and even medical matters. He had evolved into a significant headache for the British with his ingenious methods of political activism.

Did he become a party to complicated discrimination himself? Especially when he championed the Indian cause while neglecting the African?

Perhaps. What cannot be denied is the role South Africa played in the development of one of the most important figures in history.

AM: A long, long history which tells us how deep the connection had been between the Indians and the country of South Africa.

AS: But, as far as the 1996/97 Indians were considered, it was not too far-fetched to say some expected the match to be done and dusted by that very afternoon. Apprehensions that were reinforced by the atrocious start in the morning.

Ganguly is caught in the slips off Donald with only four runs added to the total. The scoreboard looks ominous at 33/4. The fast bowlers have tasted early blood and all of them are fresh.

AM: Laxman did not play at Kanpur or Durban. I found that somewhat odd, especially after his second-innings fifty on debut at Ahmedabad.

With Ganguly, Tendulkar and Azhar sealing three slots, India were left with two choices. They could either pick a specialist opener to partner Raman and have Dravid bat at six, or make Dravid open and play Laxman at six.

AS: Which is curious given that at the start of his career Raman himself had been a left-arm spinner batting low down in the order. He had taken to opening because there was a gap at the top of the order in the Indian team.

AM: They tried out the option of playing a specialist opener alongside Raman at Durban. It did not work, so they got Laxman here and pushed Dravid to the top.

It was a last-minute decision that Laxman was not aware of till he was practising slip catches before the toss. He got to know from Kumble. And here he was, batting ahead of Azhar, the man who had scored two hundreds in the last three Test matches against the same opposition.

The Cullinan diatribe

Kanpur, December 1996.

For the first of several times in his career, Laxman was dropped. A crucial half-century in the debut Test match followed by two failures in the second and he was left out.

India were marching towards victory, helped by a magnificent unbeaten 163 by Azhar. In the final innings, Laxman was sitting outside the boundary ropes when Daryll Cullinan was run out by a sharp piece of fielding by Tendulkar.

As Laxman sat clapping, Cullinan broke stride, came towards the applauding Indian bench, and thundered, 'You guys are coming to Durban soon, we'll see who claps there.'

In the practice match at Port Elizabeth the Indians were greeted by a sluggish pitch.

And in the first Test match at Durban the wicket was lightning quick.

After he scored that hundred in the third Test match, at the Wanderers, Rahul Dravid admitted in the press conference that it had taken him three Test matches to get into form.

AM: I had been rooting for Laxman since his debut. This turned out to be quite a wretched tour for him. He was not picked at Durban but top-scored in the second innings at Newlands, so things were sort of looking up for him.

Then Klusener broke Laxman's thumb in the first innings at the Wanderers. Laxman faced only four balls in the match. He was ruled out of the rest of the tour, while Dravid and Ganguly did well in both the innings in that Test match. By the time Laxman returned to the Indian side, the middle order had been decided.

Barring one Test match at Adelaide in 1999/2000, Laxman would have to open for the next four years.

The batting order

The batting order for the Adelaide Test is worth a mention.

Probably to shield their three main batsmen against a near-indomitable attack, India played two specialist openers (S. Ramesh and Devang Gandhi) and had Laxman at three, with Dravid, Tendulkar and Ganguly dropping down one slot each.

Needless to say, the tactic did not work.

Tendulkar pushes Pollock a couple of times. Bat perfectly straight, head over the ball, steady, upright, and positive. It results in two braces, down the ground and through the covers. The score is hopeless, but Tendulkar playing down the ground and timing it sends a tingle of expectation through the veins of the Indian fans.

The tingle gets more pronounced. Donald sends one down on the legs. One does not bowl there to Indian batsmen, especially Sachin Tendulkar. The ball is caressed through the wide spaces in midwicket for four.

Donald bowls straighter and is still full. Down comes the broad bat, the timing dispenses with the need of a flourishing follow-through. The ball speeds through widish midwicket for four more.

AS: Tendulkar had started to score off good balls. The difference was immediately noticeable. The Protean bowlers had to change line and length and try something new. And he kept taking them for runs.

The Tendulkar fire is ready to set the game alight. The question is whether there will be enough batting at the other end to help it blaze along. The doubts increase as Laxman gets a touch down the leg side to Pollock and Richardson throws the ball up. 58/5.

AM: The moment of reckoning. The last recognised pair. 58/5 in response to 529/7. Another wicket and it could have

56

been another tepid surrender as in Kingsmead, the series handed over without as much as a whimper.

The familiar sight. The slightly slouching gait. The feet padding across the ground as if on springs.

AS: If one caught a glimpse of his face in the younger days, the tongue would be likely to stick out a fraction from the side of his mouth. With years under his belt and the moustache appearing on his upper lip, the tongue did not flick out that often. There were many changes that Azhar went through, but this is one of the more endearing ones.

These days he has migrated to the white helmet. The light bat held nonchalantly in his hand, almost like an extension of his arm. Mohammad Azharuddin, in the midst of a curiously brilliant phase of his career, in to bat with the score reading 58/5. Half the side dismissed, still 471 runs in arrears, 272 to save the follow-on. The last recognised pair.

AM: Azhar had failed at Kingsmead, but for once he was not singled out for poor technique against pace. He had scored two hundreds and a fifty against Donald and company in the two Test matches before that in contrasting styles.

As he walked out there, I wondered what approach he would adopt. Would it be a savage counterattack to replicate that hundred at Eden Gardens? Or would it be an encore of that controlled century at Kanpur?

Over two decades down the line I realise that the latter was not an alternative. As part of the last recognised pair, you could not aim for a long innings with your side 471 behind. There was only one way to go about it.

AS: Especially if there is no way of tiring out the threatening bowlers, because there are so many of them, all of them ranging between very good to great. Azhar, if normal rules for mortals can estimate him, seemed to be on a mission to redemption. His troubles had started from the World Cup. India had progressed to the semi-final after beating Pakistan. On that hottest of afternoons, Azhar won the toss and elected to field at his favourite Eden Gardens. The tactics India had devised for the explosive Sri Lankan openers worked splendidly, both of them falling in the first over. But, Aravinda de Silva took the game away. I still remember the way he kept splitting the field that day. He beat the circle with uncanny precision, and the ball kept speeding across the billiard-top outfield.

When India batted, the wicket crumbled and broke. Once Tendulkar left for 65, India collapsed from 98/1 to 120/8. The match ended in a disgraceful display of public anger, not for the first or last time at that venue. Azhar – the same hero of Eden who had often turned the ground into the stage of some of his most magical acts – had turned villain within the course of the day. Abuse and accusations were hurled at the Indian captain, relentless, most of it rather unfounded.

AM: The unfairness of that reaction seemed more pronounced when several members of the side, in years to come, made it clear that to chase was a team decision.

I was at the ground that day. Not a single spectator seemed aghast at the idea of India chasing. If anything, they appreciated the idea, citing Jayasuriya's assault in the league match at Delhi. They lauded Azhar once the Sri Lankan openers fell in the first over.

Everything seemed acceptable while Tendulkar was at the crease. Once the collapse began, the allegations and volleys of abuse surfaced. Then came the bottles ...

AS: That's part of the Eden package. Extremes of adulation and abuse. When Azhar returned to the ground a few months later, just a few weeks before this Cape Town Test match, a lot had changed. He was no longer the captain of the side. A number of young batsmen had emerged in the middle. South Africa piled on a big total and the Indian batsmen collapsed in a heap. Azhar, for the first time in his career, retired hurt – with an injury to his forearm. The next day, he re-emerged at 161/7 and hammered a 74-ball hundred, blasting debutant Lance Klusener for five boundaries in an over. That is still the fastest Test hundred by an Indian batsman.

People saw a different Azhar. The paintbrush of the artist had been exchanged for a sledgehammer. The Protean fast bowlers bounced, and Azhar went after them with his murderous hook, a stroke he had shelved for several years. Even when he played his trademark strokes through midwicket off full deliveries, he punched them to the boundary without the caress generally associated with the man. Perhaps the blow to the arm had something to do with the modified style, but it looked a lot like anger. The stadium went crazy, each stroke celebrated with rousing cheers. The full stands rose as one to applaud the breathtaking century when it was notched up.

And I still remember the way Azhar did not acknowledge the cheers. The white helmet remained steadfast on his head and the bat hung from his hand, pointing downwards. The Eden crowd was paid back for atrocious misbehaviour in the best possible display of disdain. The rebuff of the great.

I remember thinking that day that Mohammad Azharuddin had changed.

AM: In the following Test match at Kanpur, Azhar played one of the best innings of his life. On a difficult pitch where spinners turned the ball and the fast men bowled bursts of reverse swing, he was back to his artistic self, sending balls from wide outside the off stump past the hapless mid-on and midwicket. The 163 unbeaten runs propelled India to the series win.

It was difficult to predict whether it would be the artist or the destroyer on display. On this day I suppose we saw both. As I said, there was hardly an option to play the waiting game with the side 471 in arrears. However, even the savagery of his batting was artistically executed. Which was true of Tendulkar as well.

AS: Batting in excelsis perhaps, if we take the phrase out of Plum Warner's book.

Azhar's 1996 hundred at Eden, made in 74 balls, is recognised as the fastest century by an Indian batsman in Test cricket. There is some confusion about the number of balls faced by Kapil while cracking the 1986/87 hundred against Sri Lanka at Kanpur. Some sources suggest that was also scored in 74 balls, but due to the absence of reliable scorebooks there remains some doubt about the exact figure.

Donald bowls shorter at Tendulkar. The steer off the back foot is controlled and finds the gap between third slip and gully to perfection. No one manning the third man area – a major point of debate during the turn of the century. Four more to the Indian captain.

AM: Third man remains a matter of debate. Every now and then we see a snick or a bold steer through the slip cordon go for four and frustrate the fast bowlers. On the other hand, the absence of a third man may tempt a batsman to compromise on safety and look for runs.

In Tendulkar's case, though, it was difficult to take the mid-off away and invite the drive while placing a third man, at least on this day.

AS: That is what the ability of playing straight and on the up does, even when your attack consists of two all-time great fast bowlers.

Pollock charges in now, aiming to knock Azhar over. It is a canny slower one. Only, the veteran batsman has read his mind. He uses the depth of the crease. The ball is hammered straight back off the back foot.

Not copybook, but right out of the esoteric Mohammad Azharuddin book of batting. The one only he can make sense of. Past mid-on for four.

AM: This shot was an indication of how Azhar would go about it. There is little doubt that he read the slower ball early, but most batsmen would have been content to keep it out. 63/5, a four-pronged quality pace attack, India were yet to make more than 100 in that series, and it was not a shot you would expect most batsmen to play in the 1990s. But, I suppose Azhar had made up his mind that this would be yet another Calcutta. He made that obvious, too, because you could see that extravagant backlift.

McMillan is in now. Pitches up. Tendulkar cracks him through the covers. The balance perfect, the head over the ball, the body leaning into the shot just as coaches will insist. Pollock, hot from his spell, gives futile chase. 74/5. A scoreboard that shows an innings in disarray. But already the hits thud against the boundary boards in ominous warning.

AS: One could play the waiting game or one could counterattack. Rahul Dravid tried the waiting game. It was the way he played for most of his career: 41 balls for 2, including a missed opportunity. It is rather difficult to wait for the bad ball or for the good bowlers to tire when there are four of them, two great, two very good, coming at you relentlessly. You won't get a bad ball too often, and more often than not you will get one too good to play.

AM: That is why the Tendulkar–Azhar approach worked here. Controlled aggression, scoring off the good deliveries, ensuring that the bowlers cannot keep bowling where they want to, forcing them to bowl to your strengths.

AS: In fact, Kapil Dev showed the way with his impeccable hundred in 1992/93, the last of his career.

McMillan bounces. Tendulkar swivels and pulls. A stroke that he loves to play, but that has brought forth his demise a number of times. Most recently at Edgbaston the ball from Chris Lewis had steepled in the air before coming down into the hands of Graham Thorpe, bringing down the curtain on a single-handed act of genius.

A short man, according to Sunil Gavaskar, is always at risk playing the pull. But this time his back-and-across movement bears fruit. There is plenty of time to essay the stroke. And there are huge patches of empty green space in the country. Another boundary.

AS: Having matured into a cricket follower in the eighties, the sight of an Indian batsman pulling a fast bowler evokes romantic images. Mainly because few of the top Indian batsmen played the stroke with regularity.

Some eschewed the shot totally after weighing the risks it brought into the game against the probable runs. Brought up on domestic pitches, where the bowlers' back-breaking efforts more often than not failed to bounce a new ball higher than the knee, batsmen lacked sufficient practice against high-class pace to employ the stroke with confidence and consistency.

Vengsarkar thought it was too risky to pull faster men, Gavaskar admitted to not being good at it. Kapil Dev did execute a Nataraja shot in which the bat scythed across the body – it was effective and exciting in an agricultural way, rather than a real sight for sore cricket-loving eyes.

With the coming of the nineties, Tendulkar stamped his mark on all departments of the game, including the pull. A bit daring, a bit dangerous. But the adrenaline charge was exhilarating. With time he rolled his wrists and kept it down, but for the first half of his career or longer, he used to pull it hard and high.

AM: And then there were Laxman's pulls. Different from Tendulkar's, mostly because of the difference in height. As Gavaskar would say, he could get on top of the ball, which would allow him to keep the ball on the ground. It was a more controlled stroke, with less risk involved, because it took the chance-factor out of the shot.

And if the low-risk pull was less exhilarating for the spectator – safety and romance seldom go hand in hand – Laxman invariably made up for it with characteristic artistry.

AS: True. Laxman had perhaps not yet demonstrated his pull at the international level at our time of the story, but he proved to be one of the most delightful exponents of the stroke. He was styled in the Hyderabadi *gharana* of wristy willow wizardry, like Azhar. He had every bit of the silky elegance of the wrist on the on side, but was distinctly more assured than Azhar through the covers and could play the same ball to midwicket or extra cover based on the whims of his will and wrists. It would be fair to say that on faster wickets, Laxman outshone the earlier artist.

AM: The ability to control the horizontal-bat shots made Laxman the resounding success that he was against Australia, home or overseas. Not only could he keep it on the ground, he also seemed to be able to place the shot anywhere on the ground on either side. You cannot contain a batsman like that if you bowl too short, or too full, the field placement will not matter.

AS: I remember the first Test match of the following tour in Bloemfontein. That short innings of 32, made from 30 balls, a miniature masterpiece if there ever was one. It was on the fast and furious Bloemfontein wicket against Pollock, Hayward, Ntini, Klusener and Kallis.

In the ninth over, with India 20/1, Pollock ran in and bounced. Laxman, with a seeming eternity in his hands, swivelled, languid and lissom, and stroked the ball off his face. The effort was minimal and the batsman's eyes hardly followed the ball once it had been coaxed away from his zone. It sailed all the way, over the boundary board behind square leg, into the crowd. A short ball by one of the best in the business almost lovingly caressed away for six.

In Laxman's case such a violent stroke was curiously an extension of the exquisite artistry in the other shots. Timing and wristwork all the way.

AM: John Wright once called that innings the greatest 30 he had seen.

AS: True. But for all the beauty of the Laxman innings, it was crisis for India yet again in that Test match. 68/4.

Yet again it was Tendulkar scoring 155 to pull India out of the woods. Along with the debutant Sehwag. Yet another partnership to remember. Yet another renowned name alongside Tendulkar making his one solitary hundred in South Africa. Yet another gem by Tendulkar.

AM: And a gem by Sehwag as well. I wonder how things might have been at Durban if someone like Sehwag had got going in one of the two innings. A one-session stay might have turned the Test match on its head. He might have converted that first-innings team total of 100 to 200.

AS: If he had got going. A big if. With Sehwag on foreign tracks, it was more miss than hit. One century in South Africa, one in England. Otherwise the record is pretty ordinary in these countries. It is surprisingly good in Australia, though.

AM: The most special was his splendid hundred on the 2007/08 tour. Originally not in the list of 24 probables, Sehwag was picked for the tour as a wildcard entry when Gambhir was ruled out.

Even then he was left out of the XI for the first two Test matches, and was selected only after India went 0-2 down. Then the ascent began. He followed his 29 and 43 at Perth with 63 and 151 at Adelaide. The last innings came out of a total of 269/7, with no other Indian batsman passing 20.

AS: Yet another gem that does not get talked about.

A stroke of fortune flashes in favour of India. From the edge of the crease Klusener angles one in and moves it away. Tendulkar's fierce square drive takes the edge and flies past gully. Frustration for the bowler. 98/5. A dab here and a dab there, and 100 is up. The first milestone and, against this attack, quite a non-trivial one in the context of the series.

AS: In the context of coming back after 22 years of isolation, South Africa became a major superpower within a very short span of time. To think India were struggling to reach 100 in three consecutive innings against them.

AM: Despite not having a world-class spinner, South Africa emerged as the most successful Test side of the decade. The 1994/95 Frank Worrell Trophy is often cited as the series where Australia replaced West Indies as the dominant force in Test cricket, but South Africa (2.23) had a better win-loss ratio than Australia (2.16) in the 1990s.

AS: The despite-not-having-a-world-class-spinner bit is interesting. The dominant side before that era was West Indies for nearly two decades without believing in a regular spinner. South Africa had a pace attack as good as any in the 1990s. If you look at the names who steamed in for them – Donald, Schultz, Matthews, Pollock, Fanie de Villiers, McMillan, and the early Klusener ...

AM: But times had changed. The West Indians dominated cricket throughout the 1980s when there were only a handful of quality spinners. With Shane Warne, Anil Kumble and Mushtaq Ahmed leading a resurgence, the bowling attacks of the 1990s looked different from their 1980s counterparts.

By the mid-1990s Saqlain Mushtaq had taken over, then Muttiah Muralitharan added the doosra to his arsenal ... and finger-spin came into the equation as well.

Even Zimbabwe had the leg breaks of Paul Strang, and in the new century, the left-arm spin of Ray Price. And Bangladesh seemed to have a very efficient supply chain of left-arm spinners from the day they started playing Test cricket, perhaps even before that.

AS: All this makes one wonder how great the South African side might have been in the 1970s and 1980s if they had continued to play. They had a top-class pace attack and were the top side in the world when they were banished into isolation. At the same time, they lacked a genuinely successful spinner.

The isolation

As already mentioned, in the 1950s the non-racial SACBOC applied for affiliation to the ICC. Quite expectedly, they were not entertained. After all, they were only the non-white fraction of South Africa playing the non-white countries. Not really something that could be taken seriously as international cricket.

The white fraction of South Africa, playing only white countries, was, however, acceptable to the Imperial Cricket Conference. They continued to play Test cricket. The whites constituted 20% of the South African population.

From 1956/57 to 1958/59, Basil D'Oliveira led the non-white South African side at home and away, against Kenyan Asians and East Africa, in victorious unofficial 'Tests'.

But subsequently the plans to bring a West Indian non-white side to play the SACBOC team fell through. Frank Worrell's men did not make the tour due to a lot of differences of opinion among the non-white South African factions. According to some – chiefly Dennis Brutus, the president of the South African Sports Association – non-whites of South Africa playing foreign non-white teams was essentially toeing the apartheid line.

D'Oliveira lost heart. He was on the brink of giving up cricket when the famous letter from John Arlott reached him – offering a contract in the Central Lancashire League.

At the age of 29, D'Oliveira left South Africa. At 31 he played for Worcestershire. At 34 for England.

At 37 he scored 158 against Australia at The Oval. After some curious controversy involving cloak and dagger intrigue, he was first omitted and then selected to tour South Africa with the England side for the 1968/69 Test series. The South African government refused to let him in. The tour was cancelled.

In 1970 the South Africans were supposed to play in England. In spite of the D'Oliveira incident, the MCC were adamant that the South Africans be invited for a full summer of cricket.

An incredible protest movement materialised against the tour. STST – Stop The Seventy Tour – united thousands of idealistic young men and women throughout the country. There were also more conventional forms of protest, organised by the likes of Rev. David Sheppard and others. Finally, the British Labour government also intervened. The tour was cancelled.

Subsequent demonstrations led to the cancellation of the 1971/72 South African tour to Australia as well.

In 1977 the Gleneagles Agreement came into being, with the Commonwealth presidents and prime ministers agreeing to discourage contact and competition between their sportsmen and sporting organisations, teams or individuals from South Africa.

> After 1970, the next time South Africa played official international cricket was in 1991, against India at the Eden Gardens.

AS: At the time of the isolation, Graeme Pollock and Barry Richards were two of the best batsmen in the world. Peter Pollock and Mike Procter formed the most vicious opening attack. Eddie Barlow was perhaps the best of his day after Sobers as an all-rounder. Denis Lindsay was a champion wicketkeeper-batsman.

And mind you, we are talking of only 20% of the South African population from which the team was selected. The non-white cricket circuit was teeming with talent as well.

Vince Barnes, for example, was a coloured bowler who regularly wreaked havoc in the non-white Howa Bowl. When those matches were later deemed first class, he was credited with 323 wickets at the incredible average of 11.95! In the history of first-class cricket, no bowler in the 20th century or later has taken more wickets at a better average. There was also Owen Williams and others who were some of the best unknown cricketers of the world.

South African cricketers whose Test careers were truncated by isolation

Player	M	R	Ave	W	Ave	C/S
Ali Bacher	12	679	32.33	-	-	10
Eddie Barlow	30	2,516	45.74	40	34.05	35
Graham Chevalier	1	0	0.00	5	20.00	1
Lee Irvine	4	353	50.42	-	-	2
Tiger Lance	13	591	28.14	12	39.91	7
Denis Lindsay	19	1,130	37.66	-	-	57/2
Peter Pollock	28	607	21.67	116	24.18	9
Graeme Pollock	23	2,256	60.97	4	51.00	17
Mike Procter	7	226	25.11	41	15.02	4
Barry Richards	4	508	72.57	1	26.00	3

AM: Then there were the rebel Test matches of the 1980s. Like the two Rest of the World tours in 1970 (England) and 1971/72 (Australia), and Kerry Packer's SuperTests, many of the rebel Tests featured a level of cricket comparable to the best we have seen on the official circuit.

AS: Yes, the two Rest of the World tours provided some of the most competitive cricket among the best players of the time.

Once it was certain that the isolation was there to stay, some of the South African stars spent the summers playing county cricket in England. Barry Richards, Mike Procter, Clive Rice, Garth le Roux, Jimmy Cook and Peter Kirsten all became household names.

South Africans playing for English counties, 1970–1991
Ignores stints < 10 matches (Peter Kirsten for Sussex, for example)

Cricketer	Team	Stint	M	R	Ave	W	Ave
Clive Rice	Notts	75–87	283	17,053	44.29	476	23.58
Mike Procter	Gloucester	70*–81	209	12,643	39.02	656	20.50
Barry Richards	Hants	70*–78	152	11,853	50.22		
Garth le Roux	Sussex	78–87	137	3,341	28.31	393	23.16
Peter Kirsten	Derby	78–82	106	7,722	49.50	49	38.14
Allan Donald	Warwicks	87–91*	74			263	21.54
Jimmy Cook	Somerset	89–91	71	7,604	72.41		
Eddie Barlow	Derby	76–78	60	2,813	31.25	98	21.51
Kepler Wessels	Sussex	76–80	53	4,329	52.15		
H. Ackerman	Northants	70*–71	49	2,891	32.85		
V. van der Bijl	Middlesex	80–81	21	331	25.46	86	15.00
Brian McMillan	Warwicks	86	12	999	58.76	17	47.52
Adrian Kuiper	Derby	90	12	407	23.94	12	32.75
Fanie de Villiers	Kent	90	12	264	22.00	25	39.68

*Note:
Procter played for Gloucestershire from 1965
Ackerman played for Northamptonshire from 1967
Richards played for Hampshire from 1968
Donald played for Warwickshire until 2000

AM: Kepler Wessels had a long stint for Queensland, even playing Test cricket for Australia. Barry Richards played in the Sheffield Shield as well.

South Africans playing for Australian states, 1970–1991

Cricketer	Team	Stint	M	R	Ave
Kepler Wessels	Queensland	79/80–85/86	62	5,419	52.10
Barry Richards	South Australia	70/71	10	1,538	109.85

AS: Meanwhile, Ali Bacher and the other organisers worked day in, day out to ensure that the standard of cricket was maintained in South Africa, so that when they were re-admitted, they would, to use a cliché, hit the ground running.

Cricketers were wooed with great financial incentives, plans were hatched, lieutenants scoured the world trying to recruit the best. The matches were marketed with great attention to detail – the companies sponsoring the games, such as Panasonic, were offered substantial tax rebates.

Not all the teams that they managed to bring over were great. The Sri Lankan side of 1982 was a minnow reflecting their status in the real Test world. The first England side was a motley group of disillusioned and disoriented players at best, although they did include some big names.

AM: The Sri Lankan side did not consist of some of their best cricketers. Bandula Warnapura, captain of the squad, personally discouraged a young Arjuna Ranatunga from joining the tour. That had a great effect on the future of Sri Lankan cricket.

They even went under the name of AROSA Sri Lanka, the first three letters of that acronym being the initials of Anthony Ralph Opatha, player-manager on that tour.

AS: Even the England side of 1982 were called South African Breweries XI because of the sponsors.

SACHIN AND AZHAR AT CAPE TOWN

Later, the two Australian sides were decent. However, the real coup was with the two West Indian sides. Both in cricketing and political terms.

Most of the major pillars of the South African side when they re-entered the international fold had achieved stardom in the rebel 'Tests'. Peter Kirsten, Cook, Rice, Donald, Kuiper, McMillan.

More importantly, all these cricketers had rubbed shoulders with international names, including their own Graeme Pollock and Barry Richards.

The rebels who came

Season	Stars	Result
1981/82	England: Gooch (c), Boycott, Underwood, Woolmer, Old, Lever, Knott, Amiss, Emburey	SA 1-0 (3)
1982	Sri Lanka: Warnapura (c), Goonatilleke	SA 2-0 (2)
1982/83	West Indies: Rowe (c), Kallicharran, Stephenson, Moseley, David Murray, Clarke, King	1-1 (2)
1983/84	West Indies: Rowe (c), Kallicharran (c), Julien, Stephenson, Croft, Clarke, Moseley, King, Murray, Bacchus	WI 2-1 (4)
1985/86	Australia: Hughes (c), Dyson, Hogg, Rixon, Yallop, Rackemann	SA 1-0 (3)
1986/87	Australia: Hughes (c), Dyson, Wessels, Rixon, Rackemann	SA 1-0 (4)
1989/90	England: Gatting (c), Robinson, Ellison, Foster, French, Broad, Athey, Jarvis, Emburey	SA 1-0 (1)

Honorary whites

Before the rebel Tests started, there had been private teams who played in South Africa.

Through the 1970s, Derrick Robins's sides consisting of motley groups of international and first-class cricketers playing in South Africa.

In 1974/75, a Derrick Robins team led by Brian Close and represented by stalwarts such as Tony Greig, Terry Jenner, Max Walker and Clive Radley toured South Africa. This side included two non-white cricketers who visited as 'honorary whites'. They were Pakistani Younis Ahmed and West Indian John Shepherd.

According to Paddy Briggs, the biographer of Shepherd:

'The Robins tour was undoubtedly, as we have seen, a determined attempt by the white South Africa cricket authorities to keep the door open to the rest of the cricketing world and to try and present a more acceptable face to them ...

'On this first tour John Shepherd was an "honorary white" – a bizarre status which required him to have a minder in the shadows who was there to sort out any situation which might be sensitive. For example, as Shepherd spent 95% of his time in areas that were reserved exclusively for whites the minder had to smooth the way – with hotel and restaurant staff, and other guests who might question what a "Kaffir" was doing in one of their exclusive places. This was not just a courtesy to Shepherd, but also a pragmatic necessity in order to keep the tour on track. Had there been an incident in which Shepherd was insulted or abused, and had this got out to the media as it probably would have done, then the tour would have been in jeopardy.'

At the end of the tour Robins said that the visit 'could do a lot towards re-establishing South Africa–England links in time for the scheduled MCC tour of South Africa in three years' time'.

It is because of this South African connection that the Test career of Younis Ahmed became uncertain. He played in 1969/70 and then in 1986/87.

The gap of 17 years and 111 days is the third highest in the history of Test cricket.

Leading the list is John Traicos with 22 years and 22 days, whose career was interrupted by the South African isolation and was resumed for Zimbabwe.

The other cricketer with a bigger gap than Younis is George Gunn with 17 years and 363 days, whose 'record' was stretched due to the First World War.

According to Mike Procter, there was another attempt to get an England Invitation XI to play in South Africa in 1971/72, which could have seen an earlier 'honorary white' of infinitely more political value. Orchestrated by Gert Wolmarans and Hennie Viljoen, two Afrikaner media men with a passion for cricket, there was an effort backed by the sponsorship of the insurance giant Sanlam to get English cricketers including several Test players to embark on a tour to South Africa. The list of proposed cricketers supposedly included D'Oliveira himself.

In his book *Caught in the Middle*, Procter says that Wolmarans somehow managed to get the government to agree to allow the same Dolly they had stopped from playing in 1968/69. This reversal of attitude could have perhaps saved the proposed official South African tour to Australia in 1971/72. However, Procter writes that the white governing board, the South African Cricket Association (SACA), did not entertain the idea of the proposed England Invitation XI tour.

This is somewhat at odds with what transpired during the lead-up to the Australian tour. After witnessing the incredible protests during the Springbok rugby tour of Australia in 1971, Don Bradman supposedly advised Jack Cheetham, the president of SACA, that it would be better if the team sent to Australia was not all white.

Cheetham persuaded the SACA to make an official request to include two non-white players in the South African squad to tour Australia. It was not that the government had not known of this. Cheetham had been in discussion with Prime Minister B.J. Vorster in private. Dik Abed and Owen Williams were approached by Cheetham on his own initiative and were requested to join the side.

However, Hassan Howa, the SACBOC president, saw this gesture as empty. 'SACBOC wants to have nothing to do with two token non-whites in the team, like dummies in a shop window,' he said.

On 26 March, Prime Minister Vorster forwarded his government's response to the proposal of the SACA directly to Cheetham. Four days later, at a press conference, Vorster reiterated that it was the sole responsibility of the various non-white bodies to contact overseas countries and establish their own international links.

Hence, we see that for the Australian tour that same season, SACA was willing to include coloured cricketers while the government was unwilling. The complexities of colour politics in apartheid South Africa are rather difficult to understand.

AS: The West Indies sides were really good. However, Croft suffered from a back injury and Clarke remained strangely insipid. This made them a shade less intimidating.

AM: However, there was off-the-field action surrounding Croft.

AS: Clarke, too …

Croft does a Gandhi

South African Breweries announced a competition to find the 'South African Sylvester Clarke' by rewarding the fastest black bowler in Soweto with an award of R1,000 ($890). Clarke himself sat as judge in the contest.

The Croft incident was more dramatic, though.

On 29 November 1983, Colin Croft was travelling on a local Cape Town train when the conductor ordered him off his carriage. Croft had entered the *'net blankes'* or 'whites only' carriage by mistake. He agreed to move to avoid a fuss. However, a fellow traveller, Raymond Roos, protested. After a brief stand-off, Croft and Roos moved to the non-white carriage.

It was three days later that the news made it to the South African media. However, when it did embarrassment was widespread. Joe Pamensky thundered on behalf of SACU (the non-racial South African Cricket Union): 'It is a pity in this day and age when our country has come such a long way in creating a positive image for change that such an embarrassing situation should arise.'

A government spokesman, however, explained that the problem would never have occurred if Croft had not boarded a train without the West Indian party's pre-assigned 'special liaison'.

There was a faint parallel with Gandhi's ejection from the train 90 years earlier.

Fifteen years later, in South Africa to cover the West Indian visit, Croft used the help of the *Daily Telegraph* to track down Roos, the white man who had stood up for him.

> The 72-year-old man shook Croft's hand and said, 'Mr Croft, I never thought this would happen. After 15 years … this is beautiful.'

AS: There were some sterling performances by the South Africans in these rebel Test matches. For example, Graeme Pollock provided ample evidence of what the world was missing. His record was just amazing, especially given that he played till he was 42.

South African batsmen in the rebel Tests

Batsman	M	R	Ave	100
Graeme Pollock	16	1,376	65.52	5
Jimmy Cook	19	1,320	42.58	3
Peter Kirsten	19	1,192	41.10	3

AM: There were some extraordinary bowlers as well. Of them, Vintcent van der Bijl and Garth le Roux never got to play international cricket. However, Clive Rice did lead South Africa in a handful of ODIs. We also saw Donald and McMillan play in the final few rebel Tests.

South African bowlers in the rebel Tests

Bowler	M	W	Ave	5WI
Allan Donald	2	12	18.66	0
Adrian Kuiper	7	16	19.18	1
V. van der Bijl	6	29	19.86	3
Clive Rice	18	28	22.39	0
Kenny Watson	3	12	23.00	0
Garth le Roux	15	59	23.27	2
Stephen Jefferies	11	39	29.92	0
Brian McMillan	4	10	31.20	0
Alan Kourie	16	38	33.60	3

AS: Donald actually destroyed the English batting with 4-30 and 4-29 in the final rebel Test match at Wanderers. In the first innings he took four wickets, McMillan two and Richard Snell four. In the second, Donald got four, Snell and McMillan two each.

I remember watching Donald bowl at the Eden in 1991, the first ODI on re-admission. The first delivery thudded into the gloves of Richardson and made nearly 100,000 people gasp in unison. It was the fastest we had ever seen, and most had seen Marshall in 1983 and Patterson in 1987. Off his fifth ball Shastri was caught behind. In his second over Manjrekar was bowled. Tendulkar walked in at 3/2 and steadied the ship with a brilliant 62, while Amre played an excellent hand on debut.

India won, but not before Donald had made the world sit up and take notice: 5-29 off 8.4 overs. India overhauled the small total of 177 by a rather uncomfortable margin of three wickets.

AM: My first shock was registered even before Donald ran in to bowl his first ball. Given the rudimentary mainstream coverage of South African cricket in India, few in the stands had ever heard of him. We had heard of Rice and Wessels – the latter because he had toured India with Australia – but that was about it.

Richardson and the second slip stood at least the length of the pitch away from the stumps. The first slip, further behind. The distance seemed even more ridiculous because I had a seat roughly behind cover point. And then Donald ran in, tall, blonde, zinc oxide smeared across his face ... it was intimidating.

A seat from that angle meant that I could not spot the first few deliveries Donald bowled, definitely not the ones that got Shastri and Manjrekar, two batsmen who had earned a reputation of setting up a tent at the crease. All I could see were minuscule puffs of dust where the ball landed, and – poof!

Marshall and Holding might have been distant memories for some at the ground, but Patterson had played there just four years ago. Whether Donald on that day was quicker than Patterson is not something one can be certain about from that distance, but he definitely seemed at least as quick.

More importantly, Patterson, unlike Donald, was a known terror. Donald erupted into the scene out of nowhere.

AS: Thankfully, age was on his side. Donald was just 25 when South Africa were re-admitted, hence he could play 72 Test matches. With 330 wickets at 22.25 he ended as one of the greatest fast bowlers ever. But if he had started at 21 or so like most other fast bowlers, he might have had another 100 to 150 Test wickets.

The same with Graeme Pollock, I guess, a great career truncated at the other end. If we combine his official Tests and rebel Tests, his career reads 3,632 runs at 62.62 with 12 hundreds from 39 matches. That would be more fitting for a man with his incredible abilities. But then, it was all for a greater cause as he himself says.

AM: While the records of several great cricketers have been compromised, there cannot be a case for granting official status to the rebel Tests.

However, there are definitely lots of reasons for the two Rest of the World series in the early 1970s, in England and Australia, being deemed official Test matches. Granting these matches Test status would have sent out the message that the battle was against the government and its policies, not the cricketers per se, definitely not if they played under another banner.

AS: The England versus Rest of the World series of 1970, arranged as a replacement of the cancelled South Africa tour, was at first given Test status. It was also noted in *Wisden* as such. The 1971 *Wisden* notes Colin Cowdrey becoming the highest aggregate run-scorer in Test cricket, and Eddie Barlow the newest bowler to perform a Test hat-trick. All due to what they did in those matches. But all these records were rolled back.

AM: Thankfully they returned that Test cap to poor Alan Jones. The career record still reads zero Tests, though.

AS: It makes for curious reading. There is something else that's curious. The Rest of the World Tests were not granted Test status. At the same time, the ban was supposed to be against the apartheid regime. The South Africans had left the Commonwealth in 1961 on becoming a republic and according to the ICC regulations none of the Test matches they played from 1961 to 1970 should have been official Tests. But the ICC refused to take a definite decision on the issue, and the New Zealand, Australia and England boards continued to treat the representative matches as Tests. Dennis Brutus, then the president of SAN-ROC (South African Non-Racial Olympic Committee), never tired of pointing that out.

After they left the Commonwealth, their membership was invalid. And the decision of the ICC, put to vote, was deadlocked at 3-3. Australia, England and New Zealand on one side, India, Pakistan and West Indies on the other. Not for the last time divided along colour lines. South Africa did not have voting powers.

But the nudge-nudge, wink-wink attitude of the white boards ensured that Test status continued. The standard response to related queries was that 'sport and politics should not be mixed'.

All the bans leading to the Gleneagles Agreement had nothing to do with politics. It was a moral and a human issue. Normal sporting relations could not be continued in an abnormal society.

The abnormal society created by legalised apartheid

Here is a list of legislations enforced by the South African government after 1948.

Prohibition of Mixed Marriages Act (1949)

Prohibited marriage between white people and people of other races.

Immorality Amendment Act (1950)

Prohibited adultery, attempted adultery or related immoral acts (extra-marital sex) between white and black people.

Population Registration Act (1950)

Led to the creation of a national register in which every person's race was recorded. In order to categorise mixed-race individuals, evaluation of skin colour and ridiculous examinations (such as pencil test for hair) were carried out.

Group Areas Act (1950)

Ensured different residential areas for different races, often enforced through forced removal.

Suppression of Communism Act (1950)

Outlawed communism and the Communist Party in

South Africa. Communism was defined so broadly that it covered any call for radical change.

Bantu Building Workers Act (1951)

Allowed black people to be trained as artisans in the building trade but they had to work within an area designated for blacks.

Separate Representation of Voters Act (1951)

Together with the 1956 amendment, this Act led to the removal of coloureds from the common voters' roll.

Prevention of Illegal Squatting Act (1951)

Gave the Minister of Native Affairs power to remove blacks from public or privately owned land to establishment resettlement camp.

Bantu Authorities Act (1951)

Provided for the establishment of black homelands and regional authorities and abolished the Native Representative Council.

Natives Laws Amendment Act (1952)

Narrowed the definition of the category of blacks who had the right of permanent residence in towns.

Abolition of Passes and Coordination of Documents (1952)

Commonly known as the Pass Laws, it forced black people to carry identification with them at all times. No black person could leave a rural area for an urban one without a permit from the local authorities. On arrival in an urban area a permit to seek work had to be obtained within 72 hours.

Native Labour (Settlement of Disputes) (1953)
Prohibited strike action by blacks.

Bantu Education Act (1953)
The aim was to prevent Africans receiving an education that would lead them to aspire to positions they wouldn't be allowed to hold in society.

Reservation of Separate Amenities Act (1953)
Forced segregation in all public amenities, public buildings, and public transport with the aim of eliminating contact between whites and other races. The country was divided by 'Europeans Only' and 'Non-Europeans Only' signs.

Group Areas Development Act (1955)
Excluded non-whites from living in the most developed areas.

Natives (Prohibition of Interdicts) (1956)
Denied black people the option of appealing to the courts against forced removals.

Bantu Investment Corporation (1959)
Provided for the creation of financial, commercial, and industrial schemes in areas designated for black people.

Extension of University Education (1959)
Put an end to black students attending white universities (mainly the universities of Cape Town and Witwatersrand).

Promotion of Bantu Self-Government Act (1959)
Classified black people into eight ethnic groups.

Coloured Persons Communal Reserves Act (1961)
Ensured lowering wages by denying Africans rights within urban areas and by keeping their families and dependants on subsistence plots in the reserves.

Urban Bantu Councils Act (1961)
Created black councils in urban areas that were supposed to be tied to the authorities running the related ethnic homeland.

Terrorism Act (1967)
Allowed for indefinite detention without trial and established BOSS, the notorious Bureau of State Security.

Bantu Homelands Citizens Act (1970)
Compelled all black people to become a citizen of the homeland that responded to their ethnic group.

Before the Nationalist Party took complete power in 1948, there were other laws as well.
The Natives Land Act (1913)
Made it illegal for blacks to purchase or lease land from whites except in reserves; this restricted black occupancy to less than 88%t of South Africa's land.

The Natives (Urban Areas) Act (1923)
Laid the foundations for residential segregation in urban areas.

AM: But soon sports and 'politics' could no longer be kept separate. Things changed by the end of the 1960s, albeit not universally. The only surprising aspect of the eventual ban was how long it took them.

AS: Well, not everyone was happy with the ban. The parameters of normality were very different in those glorious old days. Amateurs and professionals had different rules and facilities till the early 1960s. The professional Len Hutton leading England still raised eyebrows in the mid-1950s. Women were not allowed in the Lord's pavilion before 1998.

Harold Wilson did speak of Winds of Change in his 1960 speech in Cape Town, but the Long Rooms of the archaic cricket world were not really well known for opening their glass windows and letting the same winds of change blow in.

Louis Duffus and posterity

When the 1968/69 MCC tour was cancelled because the South African government would not allow Basil D'Oliveira as a member of the visiting side, veteran cricket writer Louis Duffus wrote: 'Posterity will surely marvel how a player, helped to go overseas by the charitable gesture of white contemporaries, could be the cause of sending the cricket of his benefactors crashing into ruins.'

South Africa operated based on a different world view. So did some of their cricketing cronies.

Klusener bowls from wide of the crease again. The ball is a wee bit overpitched. Down comes Tendulkar's bat, perfectly straight.

In a flash it is past Azhar and speeding away to the boundary. A study in perfection. 106/5.

AS: Those down-the-ground strokes were harbingers of a gem in the offing. Tendulkar timing his drives was always an ominous sign.

Paul Adams has been spending his time idling in the field. He has got rid of the nightwatchman and since then the pacemen have had the ball. Now with the partnership nearing 50, the left-armer is reintroduced.

AM: This South African pace attack was world-class. At Durban, they went in without a specialist spinner. They needed only 73.2 overs to bowl India out twice. Donald had bowled 27.1 of these and Pollock 20. They did not need a spinner.

Here they left out Gibbs for Adams but had used him so far just to take out the nightwatchman. But with the two men looking to counterattack for the first time in the series, they had to call upon the slow bowler.

AS: At the Eden, the South Africans had kept bowling short and Azhar had kept hooking and pulling them. However, he did fall to a pull shot in the first Test match at Durban. Considering all that, it is indeed slightly surprising that they did not bounce him that much in this innings.

Adams runs in with that curious action that is a coach's nightmare. The ball is overpitched. Tendulkar caresses it past cover, between the two South African opening batsmen Kirsten and Hudson. They sprint after the ball, a long-distance race. Hudson from mid-off reaches it first. Tendulkar takes three. It is his fifty. Off 68 balls in just a shade more than one and a half hours. Seven boundaries. 112/5.

AS: His third 50-plus innings in South Africa. A hundred and a fifty in his first tour, a slightly disappointing trip. The first hundred, at Johannesburg in 1992/93, though, if you remember, was yet another single-handed effort. Yet another forgotten masterpiece that was not beamed back to Indian television sets. 111 from that usual 27/2. Ninth out at 212. The next highest in the innings was Kapil with 25.

That was the match when India had to score 303 on the final day, all wickets standing. And Ravi Shastri batted for three and a quarter hours for his 29. India finished on 141/4 batting all through the final day.

AM: Shastri's performance in that series has almost no parallel in Test cricket, even keeping in mind the likes of Bruce Edgar or Chris Tavaré. He scored 59 runs in the entire series but faced 412 balls (he faced – not was at the crease for, but faced – 68.4 overs) in the process and had a strike rate of 14. With a cut-off of 400 balls, this is the lowest series strike rate for anyone. The other entries are all above 18.

He hit a boundary every 82 balls. He was at the crease for 588 minutes – in other words, 12 minutes short of five sessions. All for 59 runs.

AS: And if you look at the following match at Port Elizabeth, the Johannesburg effort was positively rollicking. His two knocks in the fourth Test were 10 off 76 balls and 5 off 68. Harking back to the days of William Scotton, Dick Barlow and Alec Bannerman.

It is strange to think that the same man struck six sixes in an over. However, he was like that. Either the slowest of scorers or the wielder of the long handle – nothing in between in terms of pacing the innings. But, even then, in that series he had started shuffling around in his crease way too much and had become virtually strokeless. The South African bowling was superb and conditions were difficult, but Shastri at the top did his bit to dig India into a bit of a hole every time during that series.

Slowest batting in a series (400+ balls, where ball count available)

Batsman	Against	Season	M	R	BF	Ave	SR
Ravi Shastri	**SA**	**1992/93**	**3**	**59**	**412**	**11.80**	**14.32**
Grant Flower	Zim	2000/01	2	86	461	21.50	18.65
Trevor Chappell	Eng	1981	3	79	418	15.80	18.89
Bob Taylor	Pak	1977/78	3	86	450	28.67	19.11
Trevor Franklin	Ind	1988/89	3	86	446	14.33	19.28
Hashim Amla	Ind	2015/16	4	118	576	16.85	20.48
John Wright	Eng	1977/78	3	107	511	17.83	20.93

AM: Having said that, Shastri's role in holding the Indian batting together away from home cannot be denied. He opened the batting in 35 of his 121 innings, 32 of them away from home. While batting in the top three, he scored hundreds in England, Australia, West Indies, and Pakistan.

And when India returned to the comfort of their home turf, Shastri was invariably pushed down the order.

That dodgy knee was probably catching up with him in 1992/93, though that did not prevent him from slogging away to help India win the ODI at Centurion after W.V. Raman got a hundred.

AS: True. When the real four-pronged West Indian attack bowled at him in their backyard, Shastri scored 406 runs at 34. Note that considering the same parameters, the famous quartet bowling at him in West Indies, Gavaskar managed 240 at 30.00.

Paul Adams in action. The left-arm wrist-spinner. One wonders which has been rarer for the spectators in January 1997 – left-arm wrist-spinners or a mixed-race South African cricketer on the international stage.

AM: South Africa's rise in the first decade of the 1900s can be attributed to their battery of wrist-spinners and their mastery of the googly. They have produced wrist-spinners since the Great War, but none of them went on to have a *lasting* impact on Test cricket.

AS: Xenophon Balaskas did win them a Test match at Lord's though. In 1935. Helped to a great extent by the leatherjackets working their own magic on the wicket.

Later Taliep Salie bowled in the nets to the 1935/36 Australians under Vic Richardson. As already mentioned, Clarrie Grimmett was extremely impressed by him. Obviously, he did not get to play because he was not white. It is said that Frank Woolley arranged a contract for him with Kent, but Salie refused. According to Brian Crowley the reason was that there was no mosque near the Canterbury Cricket Ground.

Non-white South African cricketers

Basil D'Oliveira and Taliep Salie were coloured, as were some other great apartheid-era non-white cricketers such as Dol Freeman (the Malay Wally Hammond) and Cec Abrahams.

The Abed brothers represented the South African Indians and sometimes the Malay Cricket Board.

Destructive fast bowler Eric Petersen represented the Malay Cricket Board.

('Malay' was yet another term used for the mixed-race South African population, often used interchangeably with the South African Muslim population. While from 1926 to 1959 the coloured cricketers played under the South African Independent

Coloured Cricket Board [later South African Coloured Cricket Association] there remained a South African Coloured Cricket Board [later Malay Cricket Board] from 1922 to 1959 and several mixed-race cricketers, a large number of them Muslim, remained affiliated to them.)

Among the Africans playing for the South African Bantu Cricket Board, there were also a fair number of useful cricketers before Makhaya Ntini became the first black cricketer to represent South Africa in the post-apartheid age. These included Ben Malamba, Eric Majola, George Langa and others.

The first great black African cricketer was perhaps Frank Roro – a small man with quick eyes and feet who played on either side of the Second World War. He was reputed to be as good as the likes of Eric Rowan.

Three years after the 1996/97 Test match against India, during the Test against England at the same Newlands cricket ground, Roro was named one of South Africa's ten Cricketers of the 20th Century by the United Cricket Board of South Africa. Late recognition but a poignant one.

The first ever non-white cricketer to make waves in South Africa was Krom Hendricks. A mixed-race fast bowler, he impressed W.W. Read's Englishmen in 1891/92, prompting Read to strongly advise the South Africans to take him along on their England tour of 1894.

However, he was not selected. There were suggestions of his being employed as a baggage master, but there was no question of his being a regular member of the side. It is said that Cecil Rhodes, the diamond tycoon and prime minister of Cape Colony, himself ensured that Hendricks was not picked.

And there was the curious case of Charlie 'Buck' Llewellyn. The immensely gifted all-rounder slipped through the colour bar and played 15 Tests for South Africa during a 16-year period, due in part to light skin and part to exceptional talent.

In 1986, as a sign of changing times, Omar Henry, the 34-year-old coloured left-arm spinner and useful lower-order batsman, played against the Australian rebel side. In 1992, Henry became the first non-white cricketer after Llewellyn to play Test cricket for South Africa.

AM: In fact, non-white cricket in the rest of the cricket-playing nations also has a curious history. The Indian subcontinent is quite unique in the circumstances.

Non-white cricketers: subcontinent vs others

A team of Australian Aboriginal cricketers toured England in 1868. This was the first group of cricketers to tour England as well as the first organised team of Australian athletes to tour anywhere.

However, the team, formed and coached by Tom Wills, was led by Charles Lawrence. Born in Moxton, London, Lawrence had played for both Surrey and Middlesex. Wills was born to English parents in New South Wales, and was educated in Rugby and Cambridge. The team could have been formed of Aboriginals but had to have a white man at the helm.

When Australia played the first ever Test match, in 1876/77, their squad included six men born outside the nation (four in England, one in Ireland, and one in Britain-occupied India).

There was no Aboriginal cricketer this time. Every member was of European origin – a trend that also continued in South Africa and New Zealand.

The first black man to play Test cricket, incidentally, was the Tasmania-born Sam Morris – born of West Indian parents, there also being a Bengali strain in his bloodline. He played one Test for Australia in January 1885.

It was different in the West Indies.

The locals emerged in importance over their several tours of England, but the division of labour on the ground was evident. The whites were almost always batsmen, and the fast bowlers were invariably black. And a black captain was unthinkable.

On their first tour of England, in 1900, Lebrun Constantine was the first West Indian to score a hundred on English soil. His grandfather and father-in-law had both been slaves of the European settlers. Charles Ollivierre got the most runs, and Tommie Burton and 'Float' Woods got the most wickets. All were black cricketers.

But nothing changed outside the playing field. During the 1906 tour, Burton was sent home after he refused to 'carry out menial duties' for his white team-mates. In fact, he found it difficult to get a job once he was back home. He had to move to Panama.

Thankfully, things changed over time. George Headley stood in as captain for one Test match in 1947/48 – against England.

And in 1960/61, Frank Worrell became the first black man to be a full-time West Indian Test captain. Over the next decade and a half, white cricketers faded away from the national team.

When Tony Greig promised to 'make them grovel' ahead of the 1976 tour, the West Indians thrashed England 3-0. Such was the impact of that series that England could not quite recover against the West Indians till the turn of the century.

And as things stand in 2020, it is difficult to spot a white cricketer in the West Indian international set-up.

All this was in stark contrast with the development of cricket in India. Not only did the Parsees play cricket in the 19th century, they toured England twice *on their own*, in 1886 and 1888, defeated G.F. Vernon's XI in 1889/90, and started an annual contest with the Europeans based in India.

Though they picked up cricket from the British, the Parsee teams did not include British cricketers. Taking cue, the other Indians followed.

The all-India teams have never consisted of a cricketer of non-Indian origin.

Even the earliest all-Indian cricket teams were comprised only of cricketers of Indian origin, though 'Jungly' Greig was chairperson of the seven-member selection committee – the others consisted of two Hindus, two Muslims, two Parsees – that picked the All-India team that toured England in 1911.

Greig was not the only Englishman to be part of the Indian cricket set-up. Despite the scathing criticism he received for his stint as governor of Bombay, Lord Harris's role in the growth of cricket in India is undeniable.

R.E. Grant Govan, a British industrialist based in Delhi, was the first president of the BCCI.

And Major Jack Brittain-Jones, an employee under Lord Willingdon (then viceroy of India) was appointed manager for India's 1936 tour of England – though that was largely because he was part of Vizzy's 'camp'. He played a role in Vizzy's successful scheme of sending Lala Amarnath back mid-tour.

But as mentioned above, none of them *played for India*. Indian cricket teams have always consisted of cricketers of Indian origin – in stark contrast with the early teams of Australia, South Africa, West Indies and New Zealand.

However, British cricketers formed one of the five teams in the Bombay Pentangular and played for different Ranji Trophy teams. Albert Wensley (Nawanagar, 1936/37), T.C. Longfield (Bengal, 1938/39), and Herbert Barritt (Western India, 1943/44) had even led their respective teams to Ranji Trophy titles.

If anything, it worked the other way. Three cricketers of Indian origin played Test cricket for England before India played their first Test match. Ranjitsinhji had captured the imagination of England – even beyond the cricketing fraternity – before the Great War, despite having to battle racism before his Test debut.

And as cricket entered the Bradman era, both Duleepsinhji and the Nawab of Pataudi Sr emulated Ranji by scoring hundreds on their Ashes debut – as would Raman Subba Row, the fourth man of Indian origin to play Test cricket for England.

Incidentally, Ranji was tipped to be a part of Lord Hawke's 1895/96 team to tour South Africa. According to André Odendaal's *Cricket and Conquest* he was discouraged from going on the tour based on a quiet diplomatic word, and recommended his great friend C.B. Fry instead.

Ranji's brilliant nephew Duleep managed to play one Test match for England against the visiting South Africans in 1929. After that he was not picked in the series, or even for the Gentlemen against the tourists. It led his coach, the former South African great Aubrey Faulkner, to remark scathingly about the blemish on English cricket.

The following summer, with over 400 runs in the Ashes series, including a superlative 173 at Lord's, Duleep was a virtual certainty in the English side. However, it was Maurice Turnbull who was chosen for the middle-order spot Duleep should have occupied when England toured South Africa that 1930/31 summer. Duleep was sidelined with supposed 'illness'.

In many ways, the Indian prince was a precursor of Basil D'Oliveira.

The early days of Test cricket in India, thus, were significantly different from Ausralia, New Zealand, South Africa or West Indies. The other teams were invariably comprised of European expatriates and their descendants. However, not so for India. Despite being born outside India, Lall Singh, Salim Durani, Ashok Gandotra and Robin Singh were all of Indian origin. Barring the cricketers who crossed the border during the 1947 partitions, almost all Pakistan cricketers have been of local origin as well, as has been the case for Sri Lanka, Bangladesh, and Afghanistan.

Some credit for this should go to the early Indian patrons, who employed cricketers – of humble backgrounds, sometimes from small towns – to play cricket. Thus, though India took their time to earn respect at the international level, the sport cut through the social strata at a pace faster than in most countries.

AM: Talking about Adams, I was recently part of a discussion on cricketers who fell during their run-up. The list consisted of fast bowlers only.

The general consensus was that Adams was the likeliest candidate for a spinner, so we decided to ask the man himself. Adams assured us that he had never taken a tumble. How he managed to achieve this, I have no idea.

Bradman, in the 1938 Oval Test match, is probably the only known instance of a spinner falling down while bowling in Test cricket.

AS: What about when Adams celebrated his wickets? Forward flip through the air and landing on both feet? 412 first-class wickets and 84 in List A. If he did not fall even once through nearly half a thousand celebrations, it must have been a miracle.

Paul Adams on his action

My action has always been like this. I used to bowl quicker, like the seamers, when I started, but the ball would be delivered back of the hand, and released as I did later.

For me it was all about practice and landing the ball in the right area. And as I moved to spin, the focus was on having fun, bamboozling people with the turn.

So, all that developed quite naturally, the style, the action with it.

Tendulkar now celebrates the half-century with a rasping square cut off McMillan's shortish delivery. Played deliberately in the air, but far from point. The Indian captain is showing definite indications of cutting loose.

AS: McMillan and Tendulkar. I always remember them with roles reversed. The final over of the Hero Cup semi-final 1993. The drama under lights, with a mongoose as a side character. Curious mongoose that, running on to the field with religious regularity during the second innings of both the semi-finals and the final. By the second semi-final, it was being greeted with standing ovations. It was the first time day-night matches were being played at the ground, and perhaps the mongoose was not really used to all the intrusion.

AM: The Eden Gardens kept featuring throughout the career of Azhar, Tendulkar, and South Africa as a combination. Azhar led India in South Africa's comeback match; Tendulkar shared the Player of the Match with Donald. Azhar led again, with bat and otherwise, in the Hero Cup semi-final, before Tendulkar stole the show with the final over.

And yet again, with Tendulkar as captain, Azhar arrogantly bludgeoned the South Africans, twice in the same Test match, with an injured arm.

It is now that Nelson Mandela arrives. A picture of calm dignity in his loose, silk Madiba shirt. The most iconic image of the human capacity for resilience. Having completed his long march to freedom, he has not paused to rest. Freedom implies responsibility, and on Mandela's aging shoulders rests the responsibility of paving the path for the future.

Now he waves at the crowd from the president's box and is greeted by uproarious cheers. During that South African winter, the National Party have withdrawn from the coalition government, giving the African National Congress full political control. ANC, a persecuted, underground unit for decades, is at the helm, led by this man who spent 27 years of his life in prison.

In front of him one sees former Indian captain Dilip Vengsarkar, his face breaking into a wide smile in proximity of the great man.

Nelson Mandela

Born in 1918, brought up as a Xhosa lad by a Thembu regent after the death of his own father, he was expelled from Fort Hare College for protesting about the quality of food. He later obtained a degree in law at Witwatersrand University after running away from home to escape a forced marriage.

Thereafter came his involvement with the ANC.

He tasted his first prison cell in 1952, during the Defiance Campaign. The first ban was handed out the same year. That same eventful year he established the first ever African law firm, Mandela & Tambo.

Charged with treason in 1956, Mandela was acquitted after an interminably long trial in March 1961 and went on the run. Nicknamed Black Pimpernel because of his various disguises, he appeared at every important gathering and disappeared thereafter.

At the pan-African conference in Addis Ababa in 1962, his speech was sparkling: 'The freedom movement in South Africa believes that hard and swift blows should be delivered with the full weight of the masses of the people, who alone furnish us with one absolute guarantee that the freedom flames now burning in the country shall never be extinguished.'

On 5 August 1962, back in South Africa, he was driving through the Natal countryside dressed in a chauffeur's uniform when he was arrested at Howick. His life on the run had ended after 17 months.

On 20 April 1964, from the dock of the defendant, Nelson Mandela talked for three hours. It was a speech reviewed by two of his friends – the renowned authors Anthony Sampson and Nadine Gordimer. It ended:

'During my lifetime I have dedicated my life to this struggle of the African people. I have fought against white domination, and I have fought against black domination. I have cherished the ideal of a democratic and free society in which all people will live together in harmony and with equal opportunities. It is an ideal for which I hope to live and to see realised. But, My Lord, if it needs to be, it is an ideal for which I am prepared to die.'

On 12 July 1964 Mandela was found guilty on four counts of conspiracy and sabotage by Judge Quartus de Wet. Along with the other defendants he was flown to Robben Island where the guards gleefully informed him: 'This is where you'll die.' Mandela was to remain there for the next 18 years, in a ten-foot by six-foot cell, with three blankets and a straw mat.

In 1982, Nelson Mandela was moved from Robben Island to the Pollsmoor Prison near Cape Town.

In 1986, he was visited in the prison by former Australian prime minister Malcolm Fraser. Mandela's first question was, 'Tell me Mr Fraser, is Don Bradman still alive?'

When Mandela was released from prison in 1990, Fraser presented him with an autographed bat. The inscription read: 'To Nelson Mandela in recognition of a great unfinished innings – Don Bradman.'

AS: When I spoke to Dilip Vengsarkar years later, he said:

'I was reporting for some Indian newspapers ... I had played in other countries, but I had not played in South Africa ever, so it was a great experience for me. I only played against the South Africans in the Masters Cup in Bombay in 1994/95. I also scored a hundred against them.

'When I was in South Africa for the 1996/97 tour, I found the people in the country to be very friendly. There were a lot of Indians ... and they often invited me to their places.

'I was sitting in the South Africa Cricket Board president's box when Nelson Mandela came in. He stayed for an hour or so. It was great meeting him, because I had heard so much about him, his fight against apartheid.'

Masters Cup 1994/95, Bombay

India Masters vs South Africa Masters, Brabourne Stadium 1994/95 (45-over match): India Masters 280/7 (K. Srikkanth 85, Dilip Vengsarkar 105, Yashpal Sharma 39, Clive Rice 3-42) beat **South Africa Masters** 218/6 (Henry Fotheringham 44, Graeme Pollock 79*) by 62 runs.

In the final of the Masters Cup, India played West Indies. Vengsarkar scored 105 not out, slamming three consecutive sixes off Viv Richards.

For a number of Indian cricketers, including Vengsarkar, Sunil Gavaskar, Mohinder Amarnath, Karsan Ghavri, Madan Lal and others, that was the only time they played the South Africans. Vengsarkar did feature in one ODI against them during South Africa's epochal 1991 tour, but he did not get his turn to bat. By the time South Africa resumed Test cricket he had retired.

It is a pity.

There could have been plenty of such battles. Clive Rice bowling to Dilip Vengsarkar in an official Test match, Mike Procter to Sunil Gavaskar.

However, sometimes the Indian cricketers came up against a solitary South African when playing an English county during the Test tours. Gavaskar did open the Rest of the World innings with Hylton Ackerman in Australia in 1971/72. But that was about all interactions that they had at the international level.

Paul Adams runs in. Or whatever he does when he bowls. His curious route between the umpire and the stumps, the duck of the head, the whirl of the bowling arm, the left leg raised in an anatomical aberration of a posture. Azharuddin tucks him away to deep fine leg for a couple. Till now he has been the quieter of the two. That is about to change.

AS: What is it that makes left-arm wrist-spinners such a rarity in cricket? There are off-break bowlers and there are leg-break bowlers. There are an enormous number of left-arm orthodox spinners. But when it comes to left-arm wrist spin, we are down to less than once in a blue moon.

AM: First, there are significantly fewer left-arm bowlers than right-arm bowlers, and fewer wrist-spinners than finger-spinners. Left-arm wrist-spinners, thus, being the intersection of the two smaller sets (left-arm and wrist-spin), are very few in number.

But there is more. I have a theory. A quality leg-spinner is, by common consensus, more difficult to play for a right-handed batsman because the ball leaves the latter.

However, when it comes to left-arm bowling, the wrist-spinners actually bring the ball in to the right-hander, which makes them a less dangerous threat than left-arm finger-spinners. Of course, a potent googly helps.

Thus, the left-arm wrist-spinners who rise through the ranks almost always (a) are extremely good, or (b) bowl something else as well, or (c) have some credibility with the bat, or (d) face little competition from spinners of other 'genres' when it comes to a spot in the side.

AS: True. Puss Achong, Chuck Fleetwood-Smith, Lindsay Kline, Adams and Kuldeep Yadav belong to the first group. Sobers, I guess, fulfils all the categories.

AM: Kline was a better bowler than he gets credit for. A sub-23 average is no joke. Unfortunately, he is remembered more for his two outings at No. 11 – this, despite him never managing 40 even at first-class level.

AS: Kline had a deceptive googly. He performed the hat-trick in South Africa in 1957/58, ending the Cape Town Test with the last three balls. He first dismissed Eddie Fuller and Hugh Tayfield. Then he decided to bowl the normal delivery to No. 11 Neil Adcock, the ball that spun in, before changing his mind at the last moment. The googly took Adcock's edge and went to one Robert Simpson at slip (they had still not started calling him 'Bobby').

AM: Johnny Wardle turned to wrist spin specifically for the hard wickets of Australia and South Africa, otherwise he was an orthodox left-arm spinner. In spite of his success with his wrist spin in South Africa, Wardle was often asked to revert back to his normal finger spin by the rather conservative captain Peter May.

AS: There have been quite a few part-timers (group c) like Denis Compton, Roy Fredericks, Michael Bevan and so on.

Men like Jack Walsh and George Tribe were extraordinary, but they did not play too many Test matches. Walsh played none, Tribe just three.

AM: The advent of limited-overs cricket, especially Twenty20, gives batsmen little time to adjust to new bowlers, especially if they are of a type they are not used to facing.

The novelty factor brings them more and more into the equation. It started with Brad Hogg, who played franchise cricket well into his forties. And the likes of Lakshan Sandakan and Tabraiz Shamsi have now joined the fray.

Had there been no Ashwin or Jadeja, Kuldeep Yadav would have played more Tests, though at some point India will play all three.

It is worth a mention that Afghanistan fielded four spinners during their historic Test win against Bangladesh at Chittagong in 2019: leg-spinners Rashid Khan and Qais Ahmad, off-spinner Mohammad Nabi, and left-arm wrist-spinner Zahir Khan.

Paul Adams himself agrees with this assessment

I am not sure why there have been so few left-arm wrist-spinners who have come through at the highest level. Perhaps it is because bowlers essentially look to turn the ball away from right-handed batsmen.

However, now with Twenty20, people are searching for the unusual factor in bowling and there may be more bowlers of this sort making their mark.

As for my own bowling, there was never any question in my mind. I picked up the ball and started bowling it like this from the back of my hand.

AS: Curiously, the first known non-white Test cricketer of South Africa, Buck Llewellyn, was also reputed to bowl a bit of left-arm wrist spin. Of course, he was primarily a medium-pacer and a hard-hitting left-handed batsman. But he picked up the art of back-of-the-hand deliveries during the early days of the googly, from Reggie Schwarz and the others who had been trying it out.

Buck Llewellyn was born in Maritzburg to a white father and black mother ... possessing a skin light enough to slip through the segregation net. It is still not very clear how that happened. He played 15 Tests for South Africa from 1895 to 1912, but in between played most of his cricket for Hampshire, having migrated to the *relatively* tolerant England.

In modern times, Kevin Pietersen made the same journey, driven by the quota system, an understandable equalising measure that went too far in the other direction.

Quota system

Overcompensation?

Perhaps. It is never easy to find a balancing act to redress the unthinkably evil effects of the apartheid regime.

In an interview with Arunabha in 2013, the late Clive Rice said: 'There are a lot of political issues. I was lucky I went and played in England. I played with Imran Khan, Joel Garner, Sylvester Clarke. They were all my mates. In sports you earn your respect. But you see these politicians today; they never earned their respect in cricket. People don't respect them anyway. They come in with their own political agenda. That is why the likes of Kevin Pietersen and Jonathan Trott go overseas and refuse to put up with this nonsense. In the end, the cricket team suffers.'

Pietersen's father Jannie is Afrikaner, but importantly his mother Penny is English. It was this link to the mother country that breathed life into his rather stagnating career and enabled him to play international cricket.

When a young all-rounder by the name of Gulam Bodi (incidentally a batting all-rounder who bowled left-arm wrist spin) was chosen in his place for the first team, Pietersen flung a bottle across the Natal dressing room and shouted, 'I'm leaving.'

This coincided with the offer from Rice, who had once selected him for South Africa Schools. Rice, then the coach of Nottinghamshire, invited him to join the county cricket team.

Pietersen, if we are to go by his first autobiography, did make a final attempt to continue his career in

South Africa. His mentors and well-wishers, including South African captain Shaun Pollock, advised him to try his luck in England. However, his coach Graham Ford arranged a meeting with Ali Bacher. Pietersen flew to Johannesburg with his father to meet the supremo of the United Cricket Board of South Africa (UCBSA).

Pietersen writes: 'Bacher was rude to me in that meeting, and rude to my dad ... It was like he was trying to show his authority over us straight away ... [he] said soon the quota system would stop and that selection would go back to being on merit. So I said, "Dr Bacher, does that mean that, say next year, if the black and coloured players are not good enough, will Natal field an all-white side?"

'"No," he said. "They will be good enough and will play."'

It was this moment that decided the future. He made his way to England and started playing for Nottinghamshire, on a three-year contract from 2001.

He ended with more than 8,000 runs in Test cricket at an average of 47, with 23 hundreds. Runs that could have been scored for South Africa. Runs that made him one of the greatest batsmen to play for England.

Apart from that there were plenty of other murky issues, including the controversial incident of January 2002.

In a decision spurred by the complex colour codes, UCBSA president Percy Sonn overturned the choice of the selectors and replaced Jacques Rudolph with mixed-race cricketer Justin Ontong for the third Test match at Sydney.

Ontong was Cape-Coloured, like Basil D'Oliveira.

> Many must have felt that the country's cricket was going around in circles.

Adams tosses it up. Trying to lure Azhar into playing his trademark flick against the turn of the googly. The idea is noble, to extract a leading edge back to the bowler. However, the ball is slightly wide. Down the wicket charges the batsman, exchanging his artist's brush for the hammer of Thor. The bottom hand is given free rein. The follow-through ends near the back of his left shoulder. The ball sails over mid-off and beyond the ropes. The crowd is ecstatic. 127/5.

AM: Despite Tendulkar's flurry of boundaries, India were still trailing by 400. To counterattack is one thing, but lofting a left-arm wrist-spinner over mid-off in that situation is another. By this time Azhar had clearly abandoned the mundane idea of exercising caution of any sort.

AS: That had been the norm for a while now. None of the South African players, or the spectators in the ground for that matter, expected Azhar to come out all guns blazing that morning at the Eden in 1996. But he did, scoring that 74-ball hundred. And his second-innings effort was even more absurd. He came in during the last few minutes of the fourth afternoon, and the ask was to bat through the fifth day for a draw, the score reading 29/4. He never stopped playing his strokes, ending with 52 hammered from 55 balls. He was no longer following any rule.

Donald pitches what to most would be a good length ball. And in spite of all the back-and-across intentions, Tendulkar leans forward to this bolt of white lightning and drives it to the left of mid-on. Azhar has to jump to avoid the ball. It speeds away for four. 136/5.

AS: It was not particularly overpitched. That was special about Tendulkar in these conditions. He could hit the good balls for runs with minimum effort.

A small lapse of concentration. Adams pitches short. Tendulkar unfurls his square cut, perhaps misreading the googly, or perhaps reading it all right but not expecting that amount of bounce. The ball comes off the top of the bat and travels towards backward point. Donald is perhaps not the best fielder to man that crucial position. He dives forward but the ball bounces in front, well short, and beats him on the half-volley. It almost hits him in the face. Tendulkar takes two. 140/5.

AM: Cronje's decision to bring on Adams almost paid off here. Despite his height, Adams had managed to extract more bounce than Tendulkar anticipated. We would see Adams do this time and again throughout his career.

Adams played only five Tests against India, all in one season, but his numbers – both at home (9 wickets at 29.11) and on Indian soil (14 wickets at 20.28), make for splendid reading, especially so because Indians have traditionally been great players of wrist spin.

Spinners against India (post-1980, 20 or more wickets)

Spinner	M	W	Ave
Paul Adams	**5**	**23**	**23.73**
Saqlain Mushtaq	4	25	28.28
Ajantha Mendis	6	34	29.00
Nathan Lyon	18	85	32.60
Muttiah Muralitharan	22	105	32.61
Moeen Ali	12	41	32.63
Graeme Swann	10	41	32.68
Iqbal Qasim	8	21	35.00

Adil Rashid has the best record among wrist-spinners (33 wickets in 10 Tests at 35.45)
Abdul Qadir 28 wickets at 48.72
Shane Warne 43 wickets at 47.18
Danish Kaneria 43 wickets at 41.48
This underlines the mastery of the Indian batsmen over wrist-spinners and makes the record of Adams more commendable.
  It also underlines the often-ignored fact that Indians have on several occasions struggled against the conventional finger-spinners.

AM: As is evident, if we allow the smallish sample, Adams is the best among all spinners of the era against India. He is ahead of any other wrist-spinner by miles. Not bad for someone who had not heard of the terms 'Chinaman' and 'googly' till much later in his life than most Test cricketers.

Paul Adams on bowling in India

India was a very different experience.

Coming from South Africa, you don't always get that sort of assistance. Then in India all of a sudden you are landing it and the ball is turning.

But perhaps because I came from South Africa, from not so helpful pitches, consistency was important, pitching in the right places. That perhaps helped. I was also bowling a bit quickly through the air, that was helping as well.

Every time I have gone there, even as a coach after my days as a player, my interactions have been amazing. The culture of bowling spin is very strong, it has always been very interesting to look into the mindset of the spinners there.

There is no respite for Donald's frustrations. In the following over, there is nothing wrong with the delivery. In the proverbial corridor, delivered at that scorching pace. But Tendulkar has an incredible amount of time. He leans forward, opens the face of the bat. It runs down past third slip to the third-man fence. 145/5.

AM: This was a brave stroke from Tendulkar just before lunch, to a ball he could have easily left alone. The ghosts of the Durban dismissal had clearly been exorcised. However,

India were still nowhere close to making a match out of this. The next session would change that.

AS: 145/5 is rather meagre when you look at 529/7. But the crucial factor here was momentum. The 87 runs did leave the South Africans shell-shocked as they walked off the field.

LUNCH Tendulkar 72*, Azharuddin 26*, 145/5

Lunch

During lunch the Indian team is presented to Nelson Mandela.

For the meeting the Indian cricketers don their formals. Even the unbeaten batsmen take off their pads, clean themselves up and slip into their blazers. On the ground, Tendulkar introduces the team. Mandela shakes hands individually.

Friendly, courteous, without any hint of self-importance and shaded by a floppy sunhat, the president of South Africa greets each cricketer with a smile.

Later VVS Laxman will remember: 'It was during that Cape Town defeat that I first met Nelson Mandela. I have always been a huge admirer of the great man, who is to South Africa what Mahatma Gandhi is to India. To see him in flesh and blood is an experience I will cherish for the rest of my life. What struck me were his simplicity and his humility. Single-handedly, and without raising his voice, he had triggered a massive revolution, yet he was so modest. It was a lesson well learned by all of us; it put things and life in perspective.'

The lunch break is lengthened by 15 minutes when the president, having met the teams, makes an impromptu address on live TV.

A bit more on Mandela

On 11 February 1990, Nelson Mandela was released from the Victor Verster prison. He had been relocated to a cottage at this prison outside Cape Town in December 1988, a few months after his 70th birthday had been celebrated worldwide.

The alliance he formed with the then President F.W. de Klerk metamorphosed South Africa at an unexpected rate. In 1993 he became the joint winner of the Nobel Peace Prize alongside de Klerk.

In 1994 South Africa held its first ever election in which all races participated with universal adult suffrage. Conducted under the direction of the Independent Electoral Commission (IEC), it marked the culmination of the four-year process that ended apartheid. The ANC won in a landslide and Mandela was elected president.

A few months before the back-to-back tours featuring the Indian cricket team, in March 1996, the Truth and Reconciliation Commission began its formal hearings. The mandate of the commission was to bear witness to, record, and in some cases grant amnesty to the perpetrators of crimes relating to human rights violations, as well as offering reparation and rehabilitation to the victims. The report would be submitted two and a half years later.

On 10 December 1996, the third day of the third Test match between India and South Africa in Kanpur, as Azhar moved towards his second successive hundred of the series, the new constitution was signed into law. The place chosen for the signing was Sharpeville, the site of the infamous 1960 massacre.

It had been a long, long walk to freedom. Nelson Mandela still enjoyed his cricket. In his youth he had watched visiting sides from the enclosures in the ground reserved for the non-Europeans. Now he enjoyed greeting the visiting cricket teams.

In 1994, the Australian cricket team visited South Africa for the first time after isolation. President Nelson Mandela welcomed the visitors with warmth and enthusiasm, recalling his experience of watching Neil Harvey bat in the segregated days.

Now he was at the ground meeting the Indians.

This is not the first time the Indian team has met Nelson Mandela, though.

Mandela and the Indian team – the first meeting

The previous meeting had taken place during the 1992/93 tour.

A tour that saw most of the Indian contingent travelling with passports that still bore the legend: 'Valid for travel to all countries except the Republic of South Africa'.

The Indians of 1992/93 were the first non-white team to play official ICC-approved Test matches in South Africa.

The tour began with a motorcade in Durban.

And off the first ball of the series, Jimmy Cook was caught by Tendulkar off Kapil Dev.

The team visited Gandhi's Phoenix Settlement near Durban.

And in Johannesburg, they were invited for an audience with 74-year-old Mandela.

When Mandela met Amrit Mathur, the Indian administrative manager, the great man said, 'I recognised you from television.'

Mathur was left blushing.

AM: From 2015, the rubber between India and South Africa became the Mandela–Gandhi series which they play for the Freedom Trophy.

AS: Perhaps not quite Border–Gavaskar or Chappell–Hadlee in cricketing terms. But it makes a lot of sense in the context of the history of the two nations. Yet, the associations of the two men with cricket were completely different.

Mandela and cricket

As a young man Mandela watched Test matches against the visiting teams from the enclosure for non-Europeans known as the Cage. Almost without exception every non-white spectator rooted for the visitors.

We have already spoken about his continuing interest in cricket, underlined by the Bradman-related exchange with former Australian prime minister, Malcolm Fraser.

The incredible show of South Africa in the 1992 World Cup would not have taken place but for this man. And it is not the political effect of releasing Mandela that we are talking about here, but the very tangible matter of cricketing diplomacy.

LUNCH

In August 1991 Ali Bacher had brought Clive Lloyd to South Africa. The idea was to inspire the black kids, to tell them his story, to talk about what he had achieved as a black cricketer.

Lloyd wanted to meet Mandela. Bacher got on the phone with Steve Tshwete, senior member of the ANC and later minister of sports in Mandela's government.

The arrangements were made. The very next day Lloyd and Bacher were sitting with Mandela.

South Africa had been readmitted into international cricket, but there had been no move by the ICC to include them in the World Cup. When Lloyd and Bacher met Mandela, there were a lot of journalists present. One of them asked Mandela his views about South Africa playing in the World Cup.

Mandela's answer was spontaneous: 'Of course, we must play.'

That was it. The message had been passed on to the world of cricket. Things were set in motion.

South Africa, led by Kepler Wessels, soon left for Australia to participate in the World Cup.

In February 1993, South Africa hosted a triangular series involving Pakistan and West Indies. They did not get to the final but Mandela came to watch Pakistan play West Indies.

In 1994, the year Mandela became president, the Australian cricket team visited South Africa for the first time after isolation. As already mentioned, Mandela welcomed the visitors with warmth and enthusiasm, recalling his experience of watching Harvey bat in the segregated days. The memories of watching cricket from the Cage.

It was from the same Cage that Basil D'Oliveira had watched Harvey bat during the 1949/50 tour. There was no formal instruction or coaching available to the non-white cricketers. Hence D'Oliveira and his mates watched the matches from the Cage to 'steal with the eyes'.

In 1996 Mandela met D'Oliveira. It was during the home series against England. Both men stood in their whites and Proteas cricket blazer.

That same season, at St George's Park, as England played South Africa, President Mandela arrived in his cricketing attire: long whites, cream shirt and the blazer. In the president's box, Ali Bacher answered a phone call from his daughter. Mandela asked who he was speaking to. On hearing that it was Bacher's daughter, he took the phone from Bacher and spoke to her.

Of course, the 1995 Rugby World Cup, the Invictus Cup, showed exactly what he was trying to achieve with sports as a means to unify the country.

During the 1999 World Cup in England, South Africa played Pakistan in the Super Six. Lance Klusener won it from a very tight corner with a 41-ball 46.

In Johannesburg, Ali Bacher got a call from Mandela's personal assistant. The president wanted to call Klusener and congratulate him. Bacher told the PA that Klusener spoke fluent Zulu.

Mandela called Klusener and congratulated him in Zulu. Klusener remembers:

'I had the privilege of speaking to Mr Mandela a number of times actually, and it was always a pleasure getting that call, generally from his secretary saying that Mr Mandela would like to have a chat. We always ended up speaking in Zulu. Mr Mandela used to speak

LUNCH

Xhosa, I used to speak Zulu, which were pretty similar
languages and we easily understood each other.

'It was just wonderful to know the president of
the country, he was always so switched on and so
grounded, and had the dignity to have a chat and a
laugh as well.'

Just before the start of the 2003 World Cup,
Mandela met the South African team led by Shaun
Pollock. He had a special word for every player. He
knew all of them.

After he had been introduced to everyone, Mandela
came back to Makhaya Ntini. He took him aside.

'You must go back to your village and tell the
young people that you are a star,' he said.

Ntini was not yet a regular in the team. He did not
think he was a star. But Mandela reassured him. 'You
represent many millions of people, and it is important
they know what you have done.'

Later Ntini said, 'Every time I wasn't performing at
my best after that, I would think of what Tata Madiba
had said. Most of the time, I was the only black man
in the side, and he made me feel proud of that. He
made me aware of my responsibility – that's why he
told me to go back to the village and tell people that
everything was possible, that they could make their
dreams come true.'

It was Mandela's words that made Ntini carry the
shield of his people as he stood next to Pollock at the
World Cup opening ceremony. 'It was an important
symbol. Madiba said I should carry the shield for as
long as I could.'

A few years later Ntini visited Mandela at his house
in Houghton with a couple of senior players. They had

a cup of coffee. Again, Mandela told him to remember to go back to the village and encourage everyone else. 'The whole country is looking up to you to set an example.'

Ntini later remembered: 'He used words like "leader" and "responsibility", but he said them in a way that made me feel it was an honour, not something daunting.'

The experiences of Paul Adams, another non-white cricketer, were similar. Here are his recollections:

'I have met him a few times, during sporting events and privately when I had lunch with him.

'He always talked about setting an example ... are you showing your people what can be done, a shining light, a beacon, to encourage the people in the townships. Not just in sports, but in all spheres of life, business, academics, development.'

In 2005, Brian Lara had a special audience with Mandela. Not one to show either nerves on the cricket field or veneration to famous names, Lara donned a black suit, shaved meticulously and was visibly nervous when he arrived for the meeting.

While Basil D'Oliveira was in South Africa on one of his final coaching trips he received a call from Mandela. It was an invitation to lunch.

The two old men, who had played their magnificent roles in levelling the playing fields, talked while they ate. At the end of the meal, Mandela rose from his chair, hugged D'Oliveira and said, 'Thanks for coming, Basil. You must go home now. You've done your bit. Tell your family to look after you. They must look after you now.'

AS: Yes, Mandela did have a great hand in the fast-tracking of South Africa into the international circuit, and a direct role in their playing the 1992 World Cup. But things remained complicated. It was after all, and still is, a complicated country. Even during the World Cup their further participation in the tournament remained a bit vague.

AM: One wonders what the cricketers were going through. They had exceeded all possible expectations by reaching the semi-final and then suddenly they did not quite know whether they would play.

Referendum and the semi-final

Four days before the 1992 semi-final, there took place the referendum called by President de Klerk.

The white South African voters were given the simple choice of 'Yes' or 'No' to the negotiated reforms begun by de Klerk two years earlier, in which he proposed to end the apartheid system.

As Geoff Dakin, the UCBSA president, told journalists, 'If it is "No", it will be impossible for us to continue in the tournament.'

In his *Sunday Times* column skipper Kepler Wessels urged the people to vote 'Yes' for a fair and prosperous future. But the prediction was for a slim majority of 55% to 45%. The cricketers kept their fingers crossed.

Finally, the votes amounted to a resounding 68% in favour of 'Yes'. The issue was obviously far more important, but there was definitely just a tiny proportion who had voted because they wanted to see South Africa play England in the semi-final.

Which puts the brain-fade rain rule of the semi-final in a new, rather different, perspective.

AS: Perhaps in retrospect it seems that South Africa's return to international cricket had been unusually fast-tracked. It is not meant as a criticism of the move – perhaps in the scheme of things it was one more complex piece falling into place to ensure a return to normalcy. But, even when Gatting's men travelled for the final rebel tour in early 1990, the nation was burning.

The last years of apartheid

While South Africa visited India in late 1991, marking the return to international cricket, apartheid officially came to an end only in 1994 with the country's first democratic election being held between 26 and 29 April.

Reform had been underway through the period of isolation, but by no stretch of the imagination was it a normal country, and no one but the most sympathetic members of the erstwhile old boys' club of white cricketing bodies believed international cricket should be started any time soon.

The 1970s had witnessed apartheid at its most brutal. The death of Steve Biko, the conflicts in Angola, Indemnity Bill, Information Scandal, Riotous Assemblies Amendment, banning of 'subversive' writers, Emergencies ... while winds of change had just about started to trickle in with television coming into the country for the first time in 1976 and a tiny fraction of the apartheid laws being relaxed, things were as murky as they had been.

The 1980s had been as chaotic. Brutality had continued inside the country, and ANC operatives had been targeted outside as well, from Mozambique to Islington to Harare.

However, at the same time new townships were being built for the blacks in the Cape, in a drastic reversal of the Bantustan policies. Worker infiltration laws were relaxed. Yet, the Carnegie Report showed a doubling of the number of blacks under the poverty line since 1960.

Even in 1987/88 President P.W. Botha was busy rejecting the proposal to scrap the Separate Amenities Act, ruling out any possibility of a black majority government and banning 17 anti-apartheid organisations.

In November 1988 right-winger Barend Hendrik Strydom massacred six blacks in a Pretoria street. The country continued to burn while still frozen in time.

In 1989 the ICC formalised the rule that participation in South Africa through playing, coaching or administration would result in a ban of three to five years. The ad hoc handing out of whimsical suspensions was brought to an end.

When Mike Gatting took his rebels to South Africa in early 1990, he found himself in the very hotbed of a political turmoil that he neither claimed to understand nor had any illusion of being able to control.

The *Daily Mail* screamed 'Blood Money Cricket Storm', *The Times* warned of 'Rebel Threat to British Sport', and the *Daily Mirror* even declared 'Judas would have been proud of them all'.

Decent Test caps such as Chris Broad, Bill Athey, Richard Ellison, Tim Robinson, Matthew Maynard, Paul

Jarvis and John Emburey had been lured in, primarily by Ali Bacher. As the biggest surprise, Gatting had signed up as skipper. Much to the consternation of the organisers, he proclaimed – or rather insisted – that he would meet any protester in South Africa.

Meanwhile, apartheid South Africa was undergoing immense changes. In January 1989, President Botha suffered a stroke. His successor, de Klerk, previously a staunch pro-apartheid man, surprised all with a series of reforms. In September 1989, the prohibition on political protests was lifted.

Hence, violent demonstrations and police action became features of the 1990 tour.

The first tour match had to be moved from East London to Kimberley to escape the ANC agitators.

To keep his promise to petitioners, Gatting met young anti-tour leaders during the last day of the match against South African Universities. While handing over the paper, one petitioner called John Sogoneco removed his shorts to reveal buckshot wounds from police action. A stunned Gatting responded that it was not something he could help him with.

At Pietermaritzburg, Gatting was requested by petitioners to walk through a sea of demonstrators – most of them chanting 'Gatting go home' – get on a podium and receive the piece of paper outlining their demands. Against frantic pleas not to go ahead with this, Gatting defiantly did as he was asked. Walking back to his mates, he continued on his way back to the pavilion, picked up his hat and marched on to the field to continue the game, calling his men to join him. He had been naïve, but few could question his bravery.

But perhaps Gatting's last straw was when the protesters struck where it hurt him the most.

Black restaurant staff refused to serve food to the English cricketers. The team had to be cordoned off from the multiracial dining rooms and had to use the self-service buffet. No one would cook for them.

And Gatting wanted steaks ... for himself and, well, for the team.

He fumed, he frothed. Then he steeled himself, got up and marched into the kitchen. Once there, among the rather stunned kitchen staff, he proceeded to cook steaks himself.

He could withstand all protests with sympathy, but not this. The 'steaks' were too high.

The morning after the conclusion of the first 'Test', Nelson Mandela was released from prison.

The second 'Test' was supposed to be held in Cape Town. However, an explosion near the ground ensured that the fixture was cancelled.

The Mass Democratic Movement declared: 'If Gatting can make his own food, then he ought to be quite capable of making his way back to London in an emergency situation.'

The team did return. The match at Johannesburg remained the 19th and final rebel 'Test'.

In such conditions it certainly did not seem likely that South Africa would play international cricket any time soon. But things had really started turning from the previous year, with de Klerk taking over as the National Party leader in February 1989.

While the state of emergency was renewed for a fourth year, a five-year programme was announced aimed at giving the blacks a role in national and local affairs. By the end of the year, the National Security Management System had been disbanded.

With Mandela being released from prison and de Klerk taking over as president, the negotiation process was underway. The reform proposals were radical enough to see the resignation of Botha from the National Party.

The de Klerk–Mandela collaboration, which saw them jointly win the Nobel Peace Prize in 1993, was the accelerating factor.

In July 1991 the International Olympic Committee re-admitted South Africa as a full member.

Following that, the ICC granted full member-ship to UCBSA.

AM: Gandhi's association with cricket, on the other hand, was not so direct. But, being Gandhi, he did influence every aspect of the Indian scenario ... and cricket was a part of it.

Gandhi and cricket

Starting in 1892/93, the Bombay Pentangular (which started as the Presidency match, and changed into Triangular, Quadrangular and finally Pentangular) was India's most important annual cricket fixture in the first half of the 20th century, even after the advent of the Ranji Trophy. Despite being formed on religious lines, the tournament never witnessed serious communal violence – though crowd chants of 'down with the Hindus' or 'down with the Mussalmans' were not uncommon.

LUNCH

But cricket was not the most important matter in India at that point in time. Gandhi's Non-Cooperation Movement, a response to the Rowlatt Act and the Jallianwala Bagh Massacre, continued from 1920 till the Chauri Chaura Incident of 1922. It left an impact despite its short stint.

The Indian National Congress declared Purna Swaraj on 26 January 1930. Gandhi began his Dandi Satyagraha on 12 March. India was a country in political turmoil.

Meanwhile, Lord Willingdon was appointed the viceroy of India in 1931. The following year, when the Civil Disobedience Movement broke out, Willingdon had Gandhi arrested, and outlawed the Congress. A former first-class cricketer, he was aligned with Vizzy, a key cricket personality in India at that point.

The Hindu Gymkhana boycotted India's 1932 tour of England in protest after Gandhi was imprisoned. India went ahead without L.P. Jai, Vijay Merchant and Champak Mehta.

Amidst the turmoil, the Bombay Quadrangular was not held between 1930/31 and 1933/34 – though similar inter-religion tournaments continued in other parts of India. The tournament returned in 1934/35, the same season in which the inaugural edition of the Ranji Trophy took place. Despite the uncertainty around it, the Quadrangular turned out to be significantly more popular.

However, relations between the Congress and the All-India Muslim League were on the wane at this point, putting the future of the tournament in jeopardy.

One faction (this included Duleepsinhji) wanted the tournament to be abolished because of its religion-based format. The others (Wazir Ali, for example) pointed out that there could be no other occasion that would bring people of all religions together.

Now, as the 1930s drew to an end, the British included India as a participating nation in the Second World War. Congress members across India resigned from important posts in protest. To overcome religious divide was the need of the hour. The future of the tournament seemed uncertain.

By now the Quadrangular had incorporated another team – the Rest. They consisted of the Indian Christians, Buddhists, Sikhs, Jains – basically all Indians other than Hindus, Muslims, and Parsees. The team even recruited the Ceylonese.

Who could resolve this moral dilemma? Why not ask the biggest name in India at that moment?

Had it, after all, not been the outcome of Gandhi's insistence to do away with untouchability that had influenced the Hindu Gymkhana to appoint Palwankar Vithal as their first Dalit captain in 1923?

Thus, on 6 December 1940, three representatives of the Hindu Gymkhana met Gandhi at Wardha and sought an opinion. Gandhi responded: 'I would like the public of Bombay to revise their sporting code and erase from it the communal matches. I can understand matches between colleges and institutions but I never understood reasons for having Hindu, Parsi, Muslim and other communal Elevens. I should have thought that such unsportsmanlike divisions would be considered taboos in sporting language and sporting manners. Can we not have some field of life which cannot be touched by the communal spirit?'

Five days later, Bombay Hindu Cricket Club sent a telegram to Gandhi, asking for a specific answer. Did the Mahatma want *only the Hindus* to boycott the Pentangular?

The wired response was simple: 'All who hold my opinion must refrain whether few or many.'

But the Pentangular did go ahead that season, although the Hindus did not participate. They returned the following season. There was no indication of the tournament coming to an end any time soon. If anything, it turned out to be significantly more popular than the Ranji Trophy, more so after Merchant and Hazare kept breaking each other's record for the highest score on Indian soil.

Then came 16 August 1946, a day of incessant Hindu–Muslim violence in Calcutta, remembered as the Direct Action Day. Over the next few days about 4,000 died and 11,000 were injured in communal riots in what is remembered as the Week of the Long Knives or the Great Calcutta Killing.

It did not take long for the venom to spread across the nation. The Pentangular could not continue after that. Fittingly, it ended after 1945/46, just over a year before India gained Independence in 1947.

Of course, there were other cricketing connections

There is some doubt over Gandhi's active cricketing career. According to Ramachandra Guha, Ratilal Ghelabhai Mehta remembered his classmate Mohandas as 'a dashing cricketer' who 'evinced a keen interest in the game as a school student', was 'good both at batting and bowling', and 'had an uncanny understanding of the game's uncertainties as well'.

However, Guha also points out that nowhere in his memoirs or works has Gandhi made any reference to this. Was it all a figment of his imagination, then?

As already mentioned, when Gandhi travelled to England for the first time, in 1889, he carried a letter of introduction to Ranjitsinhji.

Though he was born in Porbandar, Gandhi went to Albert High School in Rajkot, a city where his father worked as a *diwan*. The two boys (Ranji was three years younger than Gandhi) grew up in the same city.

In Ian Buruma's *Playing the Game,* a fictional biography of Ranji, there is the reference of Gandhi engaged in inter-school cricket with Ranji as his opponent. Gandhi is depicted as an underhand leg-spinning lob bowler who even runs Ranji out for backing up too far at the non-striker's end, a method made famous years later by Vinoo Mankad.

But Buruma's account, as the genre suggests, is fictional.

There is more. On one occasion, when Vijay Merchant asked for Gandhi's autograph in the same autograph book that contained the signatures of 16 of the English cricketers who toured India in 1933/34, Gandhi had scribbled his own below theirs as No. 17.

Merchant concluded that it was Gandhi's way of saying that he was opposed to the British rule, but not the general British people and that included British cricketers.

Finally, months after he was assassinated, unknown to him, Gandhi became associated with another cricketing incident.

LUNCH

It was 1948 and Bradman's Invincibles were touring England.

Devadas Gandhi, the youngest of his four sons, was in England for a meeting with Reuters. It did not make sense to him, an ardent cricket follower, to lose the opportunity of watching Bradman in action.

Unfortunately, he failed to acquire a ticket for the first Test match at Trent Bridge. Desperate, he reached out to his contacts in Fleet Street to acquire a complimentary pass.

But the fans streaming in from across the country for the occasion meant that he failed to find a hotel in Nottingham. So, as Miller and Johnston were busy rolling England over for 165 (they were 74/8 at one stage), he was travelling from hotel to hotel looking for a place to spend the night.

Then he had a brainwave.

He met the warden at Nottingham County Jail and requested overnight accommodation. While this was not standard practice, the warden might have been impressed by the number of times the British prison had hosted the Mahatma (who used to refer to them as 'His Majesty's Hotel').

So Devadas Gandhi spent the night of 10 June 1948 at the prison, and, later in the day, walked through the gates of Trent Bridge.

Laker bowled Morris shortly after lunch, bringing Bradman to the crease.

The Don went without a boundary for 83 minutes before taking control. He finished the day on 130.

Gandhi Jr took the train to London after the day's play. It had been worth spending a night in jail.

High Noon

The players walk out after lunch. The appetite for entertainment has been whetted by the 87-run association before the break. Azharuddin walks to the wicket with the same nonchalance, Tendulkar with the same busy sense of purpose.

And there comes Klusener. Sending in a nice, juicy, warm-up delivery. On the pads. You don't bowl there to Azhar. The famous wrists are in action. The flick is a thing of beauty, perfected over a decade and a half. In the air, in the huge gap between square leg and midwicket. Four.

AM: You cannot bowl that line to anyone, least of all Azhar, with the vast empty expanse on the leg side.

AS: In the summer of 2020, Azhar, thin at the top, thicker in the middle, posted a video of his knocking around a few throwdowns. A few seconds of that old magic, the wrists coming into play, the ball sent in that incredible angle past where midwicket would have been. It made one nostalgic.

The Klusener delivery is once again too straight. Perhaps not a present for most batsmen, but definitely swathed in gift wrap for this one. This time there is a greater amount of flashiness in the stroke. Most other batsmen would play it straight back or towards mid-on. Most batsmen don't possess wrists that spell witchcraft. The bat carves out an arc in the air that is almost blinding. The ball is sent between midwicket and mid-on. Four more.

AM: This was not an easy stroke to play at all. It was almost as if he had eyed the gap even before the ball was bowled. It did not matter that the ball was on off and middle. He wanted that gap, he had the wrists to do it, and he did.

AS: He could play the same ball on off and middle or even outside off through midwicket or through the off. Depending on the wills and whims of his wrists.

Klusener compensates somewhat more than is advisable. It is outside the off stump and full. The stroke is languid in spite of the spectacular bat speed. The boundary boards beyond cover feel the thud of brilliance. On air, Sunil Gavaskar is delighted. Like most Indians, he is perhaps still smarting from Klusener's belting all around the park the previous evening, slamming the fastest hundred in South African history. He wants Azhar to say, 'Hey Lance, if you can hit three boundaries in a row, so can I.'

AM: Klusener's idea was right, to prevent Azhar from playing that flick. He bowled outside off, but it was a full-toss. One wonders whether the lunch at Newlands had been adequate that day, or whether Azhar had had his fill amidst the excitement of meeting Mandela. He certainly seemed hungry for more as he got stuck into Klusener.

One can see why Allan Lamb, over a decade before the match, had commented – albeit in a slightly cruder fashion – that batting came as naturally to Azhar as fornication.

Klusener pitches up and moves it away. Azhar drives square, in the air and safe, past backward point. The bowler throws his head back. The result is precisely the same. Four more. But,

Klusener has improved on his personal record. At Eden a few weeks ago, Azhar had hit him for five fours off five deliveries. Here he has to be satisfied with four. 161/5. One hundred very special runs added by these two magical cricketers.

AM: It was a risky shot, but there was no way Azhar was going to let Klusener dictate terms after those three boundaries in a row. He had hit in the air but knew where the gap was. It was Eden Gardens – almost – all over again.

Lance Klusener on his debut at Eden and bowling to Azharuddin

I did not bowl very well in the first innings and when you walk into a man at the top of his game like Mohammad Azharuddin it does not necessarily finish well. If you don't bowl well and the man is at the top of his game it looks even worse. At the same time I didn't feel that I was very far off. In the second innings I got some inspiration after a chat with Bob Woolmer and the other fast bowlers who were around, the ball reversed and I produced probably a career-saving spell of bowling. Azhar was batting well again, but I managed to get him out. Caught Brian McMillan bowled Lance Klusener.

But I think the way Azhar played in those innings and in the years that followed was just amazing.

Bowling to Mohammad Azharuddin was worth the challenge. You bowled a decent ball outside the off stump and he could put you through the leg side. I think it is a little like bowling to Steven Smith these days. All in all, quite frustrating. Azhar was a showman and I think it used to irritate me a little bit that he could play my fastest bowling wherever he felt. I think he fed off my frustration.

But that was on the field. Off the field we liked each other's company and we still do. We have kept in touch ever since our playing days were over. He is a wonderful gentleman.

The Eden Gardens innings was special even by Azhar's standards at the ground. It is not quite evident exactly what in that city brings the best out of Hyderabadi cricketers, but something does.

It was here that Ghulam Ahmed made his Test debut, played his last Test match, and took 21 of his 68 Test wickets.

M.L. Jaisimha – who scored over a quarter of his Test runs here – became the first to bat on all five days of a Test match.

Asif Iqbal got a rousing farewell in his final Test match – though he was leading Pakistan.

But nothing matches what Azhar and Laxman achieved here. In fact, Eden Gardens is the only ground outside Australia where two separate batsmen have scored over 800 runs at an average of over 100.

One must remember that it is easier to achieve in Australia, where every venue typically gets to host more Tests than the average Indian venue.

800 Test runs at a single venue

Batsman	Venue	M	R	Ave	100
Don Bradman	Headingley	4	963	192.60	4
Wally Hammond	SCG	5	808	161.60	4
Don Bradman	MCG	11	1,671	128.53	9
Steven Smith	MCG	7	908	113.50	4
Greg Chappell	The Gabba	7	1,006	111.77	5

VVS Laxman	Eden Gardens	10	1,217	110.63	5
Don Bradman	Adelaide Oval	7	970	107.77	3
M. Azharuddin	Eden Gardens	7	860	107.50	5
Garry Sobers	Sabina Park	11	1,354	104.15	5
Michael Clarke	The Gabba	10	1,030	103.00	5

AS: Don Bradman at Headingley and Wally Hammond at Sydney are the only two entries on overseas grounds. And they are at the very top of the chart. Tendulkar came close with 785 at 157 with three hundreds at Sydney.

Green Park was another ground where Azhar enjoyed batting. Of course, Kanpur does not host that many Test matches. He played three, in 1985, 1986 and 1996. And he got three hundreds and a fifty – 543 runs at 181 per innings.

AM: Azhar played his last Test match at Eden against Pakistan in 1998/99. He scored 23 and 20. Before that, he batted seven times at the Eden Gardens – against England, Pakistan, West Indies, South Africa, and Australia – scoring five hundreds and two fifties.

Every Azhar hundred here was different from the others.

A useful but sluggish effort by a debutant against England.

Slow, controlled dominance against a world-class Pakistan attack.

A masterpiece that knocked out an overconfident England side on the first day of a series.

An arrogant, back-against-the-wall counterattack against South Africa.

And ruthless domination against Australia, where he declared with that elusive double-hundred minutes away.

In five slides spanning his career, Calcutta got to see every shade of Azhar.

Donald pitches up. Too straight. Yes, one cannot bowl there to Azhar. Neither can one afford to do so to Tendulkar. The bat is heavier, hence the stroke lacks the expansive movement from backlift to follow-through. But the timing is fit for the gods, the placement immaculate, the turn of the wrist perfect in its precision. Square leg dives to his right, deep square leg sprints to his left. The ball beats both.

AS: By now the proverbial 'where do you bowl at them?' question was haunting the South African bowlers.

Donald changes tack. The ball is shorter, on the off. Tendulkar goes back and punches through cover point and extra cover.

AM: This was the length the Indians wanted Donald to bowl. When they pitched up, Donald and Pollock were unplayable at times in Durban. But here, at Cape Town, despite the pace in the pitch, the ball was not taking off from a length. This would not bother the Indians.

AS: Donald later wrote that it was difficult to stand back and applaud batsmen while getting the stick, but this was the innings during which he came closest.

Klusener again. Avoiding the middle and leg line like the plague. Men posted on the off side. Azhar threads him through the crowded cover area. He is not as pleasing to look at when driving through the off, but we are talking about the Azhar scale of aesthetics. By less exacting standards, he may as well be casually flicking a paint brush to form magnificent patterns on the scoring chart. Paul Adams does his best, but the ball beats his dive.

AS: It is difficult to describe Azhar's off-side play. Not anything close to being grammatically correct. Not remotely similar to the artistry of his on-side drives and flicks. But there was something mesmeric even in those off-side strokes.

Of course, he was an excellent cutter. The second Test hundred of his career, at Madras, saw a barrage of square of the wicket strokes on the off side against Neil Foster, Phil Edmonds and Pat Pocock. The drives were eerie in the way there was so much wrong about them but somehow seemed electric as they came off.

AM: Azhar's off-side play could, at times, scare me. I would get the feeling that the feet would not move, he would probably be too late, the bat would not come down on time. The off stump would be visible for too long. A millisecond, no more, but long enough to put me in agony.

But the bat speed always made up for the delay, and what was more, he could hit them hard, and in the gaps.

Klusener sticks to his line, Azhar varies his. The stroke is much straighter, between extra cover and mid-off. The result is the same. Fifty up for the wizard. Fifty-seven balls, just short of an hour and a half, seven fours, one six.

AS: That was the second fifty in South Africa for Azhar. The first fifty is seldom remembered, mainly because it was not telecast live. But the Port Elizabeth innings is an underrated and forgotten gem. India struggled. Shastri 10 off 76 balls, Raman 21 off 96. They crawled to 212 all out in 96 overs. Donald, Schulz, McMillan, Matthews. As good an attack as one can come up against. And Azhar stroked his way to 60 off 88 balls. In the 1990s, he could not be bogged down. You could perhaps get him out with less of an effort than you could in the 1980s, but he would find gaps that mortal batsmen did not know existed.

AM: That innings, while special, got buried under the memories of a rampant Donald and a belligerent Kapil Dev

– and the fact that it turned out to be India's only defeat in that Test series. It was also, as you say, not telecast live.

AS: People remember the W.V. Raman hundred in the Centurion ODI because it was telecast live. So much of cricket memories is due to coverage and reportage.

AM: Raman's hundred was special because of other reasons. Days after the Ayodhya incident, nationwide turmoil had led to enforcement of curfews across India. The news, sometimes aided by visuals, often not, was enough to cripple the mood of the nation. That hundred, and the eventual win, came as a relief.

Klusener still shuns the leg-middle line. Keeps probing the area outside off. But the drives have made him wary. He pitches short. Azhar's willow flashes into a ferocious square cut. Backward of point. Four more. 182/5.

   A splendid show put on for Mandela.

AM: As we have discussed earlier, Azhar's back-foot play has often been criticised, but his square cuts were as dangerous as anyone else's. There was nothing subtle about them. The bat came down so hard that you could hear the crunch, loud and clear, even in a full stadium.

AS: Yes, his square cuts were fierce. As I was saying earlier, in the Madras Test match of 1984/85, the second of his career, he gave an early indication of his command of this stroke. And if he delayed them, he could play the delicate late cut as well.

   While the square cuts were violent, the late cuts, again, carried his usual signature of artistry.

And now it is Donald to Azhar. He too tries the short stuff outside the off. The bounce higher, the pace faster. Azhar does not cut. He gets on his toes, a bit off the ground, and guides it down, safe, secure, with a bat nearly straight. The gap between gully and point is not much. The ball races through it. 187/5.

AS: Azhar's jumps. This was exceptionally well executed, but it was not always the case. The West Indian quicks had him jumping up to the short deliveries and then ducking under them, sometimes playing with the bat held in a periscopic manner. No batsman jumped as much, and it often got him in trouble. Especially to deliveries aimed at his body.

I would say that was true till the 1996 winter when suddenly the hook that he had shelved for all these years was retrieved and unfurled once again. Made for some of the most exciting batting of the decade. Here, the jump was controlled and apt.

This time Donald bowls closer to the body. The idea is to cramp him for room, play on his spurt of strokemaking, and induce a snick out of overconfidence. Azhar stays back and drives it square, exquisitely. Poor Adams sprints after it all the way and dives, but the ball pips him to the post.

AM: Donald probably wanted to bowl closer to the stumps than he did. The South Africans had learned the hard way, at Calcutta, that one could not allow Azhar room when he was in such devastating form.

The West Indians of the 1980s might have gone for his ribs with a short-leg in place.

AS: That is what distinguished this partnership ... or this pair of batsmen. With the others, the bowlers could stick to their plan. If once in a while the batsmen got on top, the bowlers could get back into their groove by reverting to a tighter line.

In this case, at both ends, there was no way of keeping it tight. Their plans had already gone haywire. If they tried to adjust their line and length and check the flow of runs, they were dispatched to the boundary in different but equally effective ways. The bowlers were at a complete loss for ideas.

Klusener keeps it up, outside the off. Only one slip in place, the rest of them spread around the off side. Azhar waits till the last moment, leans back and steers him fine. Past a diving gully. Perfectly timed and placed. Four. Klusener's red hair adds to his frustrated look, as if about to burst into flames. 197/5.

AM: Klusener's line, combined with Cronje's field placement, are indicative of South Africa's approach at this point. The ball was not wide enough for that shot, especially when bowled at that pace, but Azhar got both the timing and the placement correct.

AS: It is that exhilarating creativity amid the heat of the action that so characterised some cricketers. Azhar, Tendulkar, Laxman …

Perhaps other batsmen would have been content to block it, or dab it for a single. Azhar just found a way to the boundary with a mix of artistry and inventiveness.

Finally, the ploy of pitching outside off almost pays off. Azhar drives Klusener, away from his body. The ball travels in the air, at the speed of a bullet. At extra cover, captain Hansie Cronje throws himself full length, gets both his hands to it. But it slips through. Klusener cannot believe it. The body language of both the bowler and the captain tell the story.

AS: Cronje spilling a catch from Azhar. In the light of what took place in the subsequent years, reading of such a play will induce slightly raised eyebrows. However, this was just a hard-hit shot, a desperate attempt to hold on, and a difficult chance grassed.

AM: For two men who led exactly 100 Tests between them, it is surprising that Azhar and Cronje never walked out to toss in the same Test match.

And yet, their careers would clash so often. Cronje scored a hundred when South Africa won their first Test match after isolation, against India led by Azhar. Azhar would burst into one of his peaks – with little to show on either side – against Cronje's South Africans.

Four years later, just ahead of Cronje's fateful press conference, Azhar scored a hundred in his final Test match – when Cronje became the first overseas captain in 13 years to win a series on Indian soil.

Azhar and Cronje: the dismal ends

Amid whispers about match-fixers, shady meetings and money changing hands, it all went down pretty badly.

Azhar was removed from the team under a cloud of allegation in 1999.

Brought back in early 2000 for the final Test match against South Africa, he scored his 22nd hundred in his 99th Test match. He never played for India again as the allegations of involvement with match-fixers became too loud to ignore.

Later that year, the BCCI banned Azhar for life. The report of the investigation conducted by Central Bureau of Investigation (CBI) smeared his sterling career, spreading stains of ignominy across many glorious deeds. The ban was contested, finally removed by the BCCI, and the removal in turn questioned by the ICC – but it did not matter to the bottom line. Mohammad Azharuddin's career had ended.

As for Cronje, on 11 April 2000, the world finally crashed through the floor. UCBSA supremo Ali Bacher was staying at a game park lodge in KwaZulu-Natal when he received a call from the captain at 3.00am.

In a hushed voice, Cronje informed Bacher, 'I have not been entirely honest with you.'

Soon, the King Commission was set up headed by Judge Erwin King and the erstwhile captain of the country was subjected to a trial in full view of the media and public.

Pat Symcox alleged that the team had been offered USD250,000 to lose an ODI. A day later Herschelle Gibbs revealed that Cronje had offered USD15,000 to score less than 20 in an ODI in India.

Finally, a tearful Cronje admitted to obtaining large sums from bookmakers and asking some team-mates to underperform. On 11 October 2000, UCBSA banned Cronje for life.

It was not to be a long ban. On 1 June 2002 an AirQuarius cargo flight crashed on Cradock Peak in the Outeniqua mountain range, ending the tumultuous life of the tainted South African captain.

AS: A strange end to a troubled life. Made stranger with what happened to Bob Woolmer a few years down the line. Clive Rice had no doubt that foul play had taken place on both counts.

This is what Rice told me in a 2013 interview: 'In Cronje's case, the automated take-off and landing signals were switched off at the airports. I play golf with one of the judges and got the final case report from him. I sent the report to a friend of mine who deals with air crashes in his official capacity. He told me how the signals had been switched off. In that respect, the case report was very fishy indeed.'

AM: According to the original report of Dr Ere Seshaiah, the pathologist, Woolmer had died of asphyxia that involved manual intervention. Dr Seshaiah would later add cypermethrin poisoning as a cause.

Almost three months after the death, the Jamaican Constabulary announced that Woolmer had died of natural causes.

Rice certainly minced no words. 'These mafia betting syndicates do not stop at anything and they do not care who gets in their way,' he would later tell Fox Sports while referring to both the deaths.

No respite for Klusener – neither from Azhar nor from frustration. The ball is short and wide. Azhar throws his bat at it. He follows the dictum of slashing hard to perfection. There is one slip in place and it flies over his head for four. 200 up. Klusener can only stand with his hands on his hips and stare.

AS: Perhaps this is the moment to take a quote out of the cricket commentator's handbook of clichés. Fortune favours the brave.

And it continues. Klusener runs in again, the ball in the slot. Azhar blasts him between cover and mid-off for four. It is the hammer of Thor yet again, the crack of the bat like thunder, the ball travelling in the air like the accompanying streak of lightning. 206/5. The half hour after lunch has thus far seen 61 runs. A spectacular show ostensibly put on for Mandela. On air Robin Jackman says that he has never seen Test cricket played like this. A while later he wonders how much these two will get if they bat through till close of play. 800?

AM: This was perhaps the most incredible shot of them all. It was on the off stump, but the ring on the off side was packed. No batsman is expected to back himself to hit a fast bowler in the air and bisect mid-off and cover, certainly no Indian batsman outside the subcontinent in the 1990s in Test cricket, definitely not after being dropped there not too long ago. One cannot blame Jackman for getting carried away.

AS: Perhaps just three years down the line Jackman would have come to expect this. What with Sehwag and Gilchrist making their debuts. But this type of batting, especially against a pace bowler by a front-line batsman, was unusual.

Mind you, during that Port Elizabeth Test match in 1992/93, Kapil Dev essayed a six over straightish long-off in a slightly cross-batted style against Craig Matthews. But then Kapil was always an exception, and he was batting with the tail at that juncture.

Robin Jackman and the Guyana affair

Robin Jackman. Nicknamed 'Shoreditch Sparrow' by Alan Gibson, although he had nothing to do with Shoreditch.

A Surrey bowler from 1966 to 1982, he also played in the Currie Cup for Western Province in 1971/72, and for Rhodesia between 1972/73 and 1979/80.

Jackman did not find a place in the side led by Ian Botham that flew to the West Indies in the winter of

1980/81. But, vice-captain Bob Willis twisted his knee early in the tour. He was called up as the replacement.

When suggested that he was in for a roasting from the blades of Clive Lloyd, Viv Richards, Gordon Greenidge and Desmond Haynes, Jackman responded saying, 'What the blazes do you know? Nothing, nothing can ever stop me going anywhere or giving up anything for a chance to play for England.'

However, something did.

On the eve of the ODI in Berbice, a broadcast from Jamaica alerted the Guyanese government to Jackman's ties to South Africa. Rumours flew about during the night. Guyana had been severely anti-apartheid for many years. When cricket was over for the summer in England, Jackman was used to following the sun down south to Cape Town, where he had a coaching job and turned out in Currie Cup matches. Down the years, he married a South African girl and every English winter was spent in the diamond country.

The local 7am radio news had categorically stated that Jackman was not welcome in the country. A potential Basil D'Oliveira situation was on hand.

The teams flew to Berbice for the ODI. However, a large contingent of press men stayed back to pay a visit to the British high commissioner. Alec Bedser, chairman of the England selection committee, was asked live on British television about the Gleneagles Agreement. He had responded, 'Well, I dunno, all I know is there's a nice golf course there.' Few knew how to interpret this with regard to the Jackman case. Neither did Philip Mallet, the high commissioner, have any idea what the Guyanese government would decide.

Jackman was not playing in the ODI and the West Indies won by six wickets. The teams returned to the hotel, with the medium-pacer wondering what was in store for him.

Soon, a man in a stiff uniform arrived at the hotel, asking, 'Which is *Mr Jackson's* room?' The notice he served to the Surrey bowler read:

'REVOCATION OF PERMIT
Under
Section 21 (4B) of Immigration Act
(Cap: 14.02)

Take Notice that on the direction of the President the permit granted to you on the 23rd Feb 1981 to enter and remain in Guyana for a period of two weeks is hereby revoked with immediate effect.

(Signed) J. Thorne, Deputy Supt, Immigration'

The Georgetown Test match was called off. Strangely, a heated argument followed among the journalists accompanying the team regarding whether *Wisden* should label it as 'abandoned' or 'cancelled'. However, there was a more than serious shadow of doubt about the rest of the tour as well.

Thankfully, the Barbadian government did not follow the same policy and allowed cricket to be played. Jackman at long last donned the English sweater. He bowled well to take 4-68 against Barbados and made his international debut in the third Test match, at Bridgetown.

England were trounced by a huge margin of 298 runs. But Jackman managed to impress with figures of 3-65 and 2-76.

The West Indians did have a bit of a problem facing his bowling, but none of them had any objection to playing against him.

The South Africans change tactics. The field goes deep. The focus shifts to cutting off boundaries. The two men push singles, scamper a few twos.

But then it is Tendulkar's turn. Klusener pitches outside off again, a bit of width on offer, and the master times it beautifully as he forces it backward of point. The field threaded once again. Four more. 231/5. The game very different by now. Klusener's ten overs for the day have conceded 84 runs.

AM: After letting Azhar dominate the early overs after lunch, Tendulkar decided to take over. One could not blame Cronje if he felt exasperated at this stage. You can handle one batsman by keeping him off strike, but what do you do when there is an onslaught at both ends? Add to that their different styles (and heights), which forced the bowlers to change line, length, pace and approach every time the strike was rotated.

Pollock is in now, pitching straight and fast. Nothing whatsoever wrong with the ball. Tendulkar moves forward, down comes the bat and meets it straight. The ball races past the stumps and the non-striker. Mid-on can only jog behind it. 'That's a beautiful, beautiful, beautiful stroke,' says Jackman. 236/5.

AM: This was not the vintage Tendulkar straight drive that would achieve iconic status in years to come. He did not hold the bat in position and watch the ball race to the straight boundary. In this case, the bat followed the arc.

AS: The ball was hit on the up. The follow-through was more pronounced than the vintage Tendulkar straight drive that did not really require a follow-through at all. It was a tell-tale sign that the ball was not as full as it was made out to be. And it underlines what we have been discussing for so long in so many various ways. The good balls were being hit for boundaries.

Cronje reintroduces Donald. Fast, furious, but too straight. Tendulkar rolls his wrists as the bat meets it in front of his pads. Right hand over left. The ball speeds to the square-leg fence. 241/5. Tendulkar 96. Azharuddin 94.

AM: Tendulkar and Azhar had both mastered the flick, but that was where the difference ended. Tendulkar's body swivelled when he rolled his wrists to play anywhere between midwicket and square leg, something coaches would advise young cricketers to emulate.

Azhar, on the other hand, never seemed to bother about such technicalities. His extraordinary wrists enabled him to pick the ball up from any line to any gap on the leg side. There was little apparent physical movement, which made the shots look impossible at times. Definitely not ideal for young cricketers to observe and learn, but some things are better left untouched.

AS: To think such treatment was meted out when Donald and Pollock were bowling in tandem. In 47 Tests together they took 397 wickets at 21.85, with 22 five-wicket hauls between them in those Tests. There have been pairs with more wickets, but none except Marshall and Garner (322 at 21.72) and Steyn and Philander (331 at 21.70) have more than 300 at a better average, and then too only marginally.

Take Lillee and Thomson, Lindwall and Miller, Hall and Griffith, Trueman and Statham, Roberts and Holding,

Wasim and Waqar, Ambrose and Bishop … all those pairs whose fantastic feats become more fantastic with the elastic properties of elapsed time.

Donald and Pollock, hampered that their bad days were also beamed all over television screens as much as their good ones, suffer in the area of mythification. But they were just as deadly.

We must remember that this was just Pollock's seventh Test match. But he already had 21 wickets at exactly 20 apiece.

And then again, the pair was up against Tendulkar and Azhar. A battle as fascinating as you can get.

Bowling pairs with 300-plus wickets while bowling together

W	Bowler 1	Bowler 2	Period	Ave
331	Dale Steyn	Vernon Philander	2011–2019	21.70
322	Malcolm Marshall	Joel Garner	1980–1987	21.72
397	Alan Donald	Shaun Pollock	1995–2002	21.84
331	Joel Garner	Michael Holding	1979–1987	21.97
559	Wasim Akram	Waqar Younis	1985–2002	22.12
338	Malcolm Marshall	Courtney Walsh	1984–1991	22.48
304	Curtly Ambrose	Ian Bishop	1989–1998	22.62
762	Curtly Ambrose	Courtney Walsh	1988–2000	22.67
345	Ray Lindwall	Keith Miller	1946–1956	23.00
484	Glenn McGrath	Jason Gillespie	1996–2005	23.01
522	Dale Steyn	Morne Morkel	2008–2018	24.89
476	Ian Botham	Bob Willis	1977–1984	25.18
371	Glenn McGrath	Brett Lee	1999–2007	25.31
310	Richard Hadlee	Ewen Chatfield	1977–1989	25.39
424	Dale Steyn	Jacques Kallis	2004–2013	25.46
547	Shaun Pollock	Jacques Kallis	1995–2008	25.99
337	Richard Hadlee	Lance Cairns	1974–1985	26.09
490	Makhaya Ntini	Shaun Pollock	1998–2008	26.24
919	James Anderson	Stuart Broad	2008–2020	26.44
458	Trent Boult	Tim Southee	2011–2020	26.88
367	Matthew Hoggard	Andrew Flintoff	2001–2006	29.11

Other noteworthy pairs who did not get 300 wickets:
Peter Pollock–Mike Procter 64 at 17.36
(South Africa's pre-isolation pair)
Neil Adcock–Peter Heine 102 at 22.08
(South Africa's first great new-ball pair)
Malcolm Marshall–Michael Holding 291 at 22.77
Imran Khan–Wasim Akram 239 at 24.39
Andy Roberts–Michael Holding 233 at 25.66
Brian Statham–Fred Trueman 284 at 25.73
Dennis Lillee–Jeff Thomson 217 at 27.21
Kemar Roach–Shannon Gabriel 198 at 26.20
Wes Hall–Charlie Griffith 157 at 29.55

AS: You will notice one thing. The Lillee–Thomson and Hall–Griffith pairings do not quite match the immense hype that has been created around them by cricket writers. The standard response to that is obviously 'numbers don't show the whole picture' or 'ask the people who faced them'. But the truth lies elsewhere.

AM: Much of their reputation is because of the record against England.

AS: As ever, numbers provide very accurate evidence that this is indeed the case.

Lillee–Thomson and Hall–Griffith, vs England and others

Pair	Vs England		Vs Others		Overall	
	W	Ave	W	Ave	W	Ave
Lillee–Thomson	103	22.67	114	31.31	217	27.21
Hall–Griffith	100	27.28	57	33.52	157	29.55

AS: This table clearly shows how the performance of both Lillee–Thomson and Hall–Griffith were far better against England than against the rest of the world. As a result, much more was written about their exploits than some others such as Boult–Southee and Hadlee–Cairns.

But, as ever, people generally tend to form their opinions based on patchy memories and things they have heard repeated over and over again … and then that idea becomes so deep-rooted in their collective consciousness that faced with contrary facts the resulting cognitive dissonance generates the immediate counter: 'Numbers don't tell you the full story.'

Which underlines the point that this story needed to be penned down.

The Tendulkar–Azhar partnership needs to be talked about, lesser deeds have already had more sound bites and will eventually be ranked higher in non-empirical nostalgic analysis … and numbers left in the wake will fight a battle as futile as ever.

Coming back to the Donald–Pollock numbers, we see they are tremendous stats. It is quite a wonder how South Africans have kept producing fast bowlers of such supreme quality ever since their return from isolation.

AM: Yes, Donald–Pollock and then Steyn–Philander are perhaps the crème de la crème. But the fast-bowling talent is really mind-boggling. The Indian context, viewed side by side, makes for some rather ordinary reading all through history but for the very recent years.

Donald, Pollock and their clan

In 1996 Shaun Pollock took out Greg McMillan, James Whitaker, Phil Robinson and Darren Maddy in consecutive balls in a Benson & Hedges match against Leicestershire. In the process he became the second bowler in history (and the first in 26 years) to take four wickets in four balls in List A cricket.

At that point his figures read a very Courtney Walshesque 3.5-2-1-5. He eventually finished with 10-5-21-6.

This was Pollock's first match for Warwickshire. When he left the field with his team, the senior overseas professional was waiting for him with the county cap. This was Allan Donald.

Warwickshire had signed up Pollock for the 1996 season, but Donald had stayed on as bowling and physical fitness coach.

In a way it was symbolic of how, since re-admission, the South African fast bowlers have seldom been alone in their hunt.

Until Pollock came along, there was always a Brian McMillan or a Craig Matthews or a Fanie de Villiers or a Brett Schultz to bowl in tandem with Donald, often two or three of them at the same time.

And as they faded away, Makhaya Ntini joined the fray, and two years later, Andre Nel. Jacques Kallis had been a continuous presence. And the trend continues.

South African fast bowlers since re-admission

(75+ wickets)

	Debut Test	Last Test	M	W
Allan Donald	1992	2002	72	330
Fanie de Villiers	1993	1998	18	85
Shaun Pollock	1996	2008	108	421
Makhaya Ntini	1998	2009	101	390
Andre Nel	2001	2008	36	123
Dale Steyn	2004	2019	93	439
Morne Morkel	2006	2018	86	309
Vernon Philander	2011	2020	64	224
Kagiso Rabada	2015	Active	43	197

Other active South African fast bowlers

	Debut Test	Last Test	M	W
Kyle Abbott	2013	Kolpak	11	39
Duanne Olivier	2017	Kolpak	10	48
Lungi Ngidi	2018	Active	5	15
Anrich Nortje	2019	Active	6	19

South African all-rounders since re-admission (75+ wickets)

	Debut Test	Last Test	M	W
Brian McMillan	1992	1998	38	85
Jacques Kallis	1995	2013	165	291
Lance Klusener	1996	2004	49	80

This is in stark contrast with their Indian counterparts. Kapil Dev and Karsan Ghavri did have a brief overlap, but it was not long enough.

Javagal Srinath peaked when Kapil Dev was past his prime. Neither Manoj Prabhakar, Venkatesh Prasad nor Ajit Agarkar lasted long enough in the format. And just like Srinath for Kapil, Zaheer Khan came too late for Srinath.

Ishant Sharma arrived just when Zaheer approached his prime, but he did not live up to the expectations early on.

It was not before the late 2010s that Mohammed Shami and Jasprit Bumrah joined forces with a vastly improved Ishant. With Bhuvneshwar Kumar and Umesh Yadav also available, the pace attack at the time of writing is as good as any India have had in their history.

Donald's delivery is fast, straight, on middle and off stump. Down comes the mighty willow yet again. The turn of the wrist, the deflection and off it speeds and thuds back from the boards beyond square leg. Exactly 100 for Tendulkar in three hours off 138 balls with 16 fours. The 11th hundred of his career and the first as captain.

'Sachin played one of the greatest knocks I have ever seen. I can recall two things – one is Allan Donald taking the second new ball and bowling from the Wynberg End. Then what we see is straight drives, cover drives, and pulls and cuts. Sachin simply annihilated Donald,' Ali Bacher would later tell G. Viswanath of The Hindu.

AS: As he raised his bat, all of us watching transfixed in our hostel lounge broke into applause. Nothing extraordinary about that. But people discussed – actually discussed – that he had finally got over his barren hundred-less stretch. Given that his last hundred had been five months and six Test matches earlier, one understands the standards people had come to expect of Tendulkar.

AM: For a while it seemed that Azhar would beat his captain to the hundred, but Tendulkar got there first, exploding in a sudden flurry of boundaries. But then, Azhar was certainly not going to take too long ...

Five runs later Azhar dabs Klusener to the off side and sprints down the wicket. Tendulkar responds. The run is completed. The eyes glance heavenwards, the glove is waved and the bat is raised. Two hours and 22 minutes, 96 balls, 16 fours and a six.

AM: The second fifty took Azhar 39 balls. He hit nine fours – most of them after Cronje decided to take the slips out and spread the field. It seemed too good to last – both the innings and the partnership – but the two men, and cricket, seemed determined to put on a show for Mandela at the cost of his countrymen. Had they batted till the end of the day, Mandela might have contemplated a transfer of Devon Malcolm's 'destroyer' tag to the two Indians.

AS: Yes, it was at Soweto in late 1995 that Mandela had been introduced to the England side and had greeted Devon Malcolm with the words 'I know you, you're the destroyer'. A tribute to the 9-59 at The Oval, 1994.

Azhar's reinvention as a blaster happened after that, definitely a post-Eden-1996 phenomenon. However, there was a distinct difference in the way he approached his innings from the moment he became captain. You must remember the several splendid innings he played in the 1989/90 tour of New Zealand and the 1990 tour of England. Before that he used to score at a conventional Test match rate, through most of the 1980s. But from that New Zealand tour onwards he became one of the fastest scorers.

AM: The hundred at Lord's was probably the defining moment. Graham Gooch scored a triple-hundred (and another hundred in the second innings); there were three other hundreds in the Test match; Kapil Dev produced one of the most-viewed YouTube clips by hitting four sixes in a row; but it was Azhar's innings that the English media went gaga over.

Just before that Test series began, Paul Gascoigne had an excellent run in the FIFA World Cup in Italy. Now, a group of fans put up a banner that ran AZZA'S THE GAZZA FOR INDIA.

AS: Harsha Bhogle later said that he did not remember many of the strokes Gooch played during his 333 and 123, while he remembered several from Azhar's 121.

Through the 1980s his hundreds came at a strike rate in the 40s or early 50s. And suddenly at Auckland he got 192 off 259 balls. Then at Lord's 121 off 111.

There is also the strange habit of Azhar of scoring hundreds in lots.

Three hundreds in the first three Tests. Three more in his 16th, 18th and 19th. One in each Test match from 37th to 39th. And so on.

Azharuddin's Test hundreds and his rate of scoring

Hundred #	Start	End	SR	% runs in boundaries
1–7*	1984/85	1989/90	46.5	43.1%
8–12	1989/90	1992/93	80.2	51.8%
13–17	1993/94	1996/97	72.5	59.7%
18–22	1997	1999/00	63.7	51.5%

* The details of balls faced are not available for his fourth and fifth Test hundreds (199 at Kanpur, 141 at Chennai, both in 1986/87)

Donald bounces. Azhar pulls him with disdain. Not exactly the best timing. At Durban he had been caught off the attempted pull. But here it careens in front of square for four. 256/5 and the fast bowler looks daggers in every direction.

AM: This was almost condescending, and Donald's reaction made that evident. The ball came at Azhar rapidly, but he still had enough time to play it in front of square – never easy when the ball grows on you at that pace.

Nearly eight years before this tour, Azhar had received some flak after the West Indian fast bowlers exploited his weakness. Dilip Vengsarkar's 'if people are frightened of fast bowling, they should not play Test cricket' comment was almost certainly aimed at him.

AS: That was a torrid tour for most Indian batsmen. But Azhar's periscopic way of dealing with the short ball came under special scrutiny. Some of the pictures of that tour made one wonder whether Azhar was hooking, fending or ducking. A jump and a swipe with eyes everywhere but on the ball.

AM: Azhar scored some dazzling hundreds in New Zealand and England in his first year as Test captain. Unfortunately, he could not replicate that form in Australia and South Africa, where the fast bowlers kept pushing him back. While the shades of brilliance peeped through – the Adelaide hundred of 1991/92 is an example – the runs dried up.

It did not help that India played a solitary Test match at home between 1988/89 and 1992/93, that too against Sri Lanka, ensuring Azhar never got to lead India at home for his first three years at the helm. When Test cricket resumed in India, Azhar was back in his comfort zone, not really needing to handle hostile bouncer barrages.

The hook had been stowed away somewhere till he copped that blow on the arm at the Eden Gardens. Then the floodgates opened.

AS: Azhar retiring hurt was a very, very rare occurrence. It happened only once in international cricket, at Eden in 1996. And the following day, with India seven down, he returned to a hero's welcome. The South Africans kept bouncing and he kept hooking them.

It was obvious he was out there to prove a point. The question is, who to? Was it the South African fast bowlers who had struck him on the elbow and perhaps thought they could intimidate him? Was it the Eden crowd who had booed him during that unfortunate semi-final against Sri Lanka? Or was it Madan Lal, the coach, who had somehow questioned his commitment by suggesting that he should have stayed out there after being hit?

For all the artistry of his batting, the hook was one of his 'Thor' strokes. There was nothing beautiful about it.

Batsmen like Laxman, essentially artists, carried the pristine beauty of their strokeplay even when they played the hook. Azhar, when he hooked, just carted the ball mercilessly.

We have already discussed the difference between his off-side and on-side strokes. And then there was the square cut, which was a rasping flash of the blade. The hook was similar. Brutal.

However, it is perhaps not a very appropriate comparison. Laxman and Azhar were both Hyderabadi and both wristy players through midwicket. That is where the similarities ended. Laxman's game was much more rooted to the basics, his strokeplay built on solid foundations, an extension of a solid technique. Azhar wrote a book of batsmanship of his own. He did not follow too many rules. Laxman did flick, create impossible angles, but he played straight. Azhar's bat was seldom anything but angular.

Donald follows the bouncer with a yorker. An age-old combination. But it does not pitch and reaches Azhar on the full. Worse, it is on the pads. The angled bat comes down, the wrists conjure up the trick they have performed thousands of times. The ball speeds to the midwicket boundary. 260/5 and the 200 partnership is up.

AM: The bouncer-yorker ploy did not work. Reaching to the pitch of the ball was never a necessary condition for Azhar to keep out an overpitched ball, even place it for runs. Those wrists allowed him to play this one wide of midwicket with ridiculous ease – but then, this is something he could possibly have played with his eyes closed.

AS: In any case, the bouncer-yorker combination generally works if the former shakes the batsman and makes him remain stuck on the back foot. Not if the bouncer has been dispatched to the country with a considerable amount of disdain. And in any case, for Azhar often getting stuck on his crease did not matter. The bat came down and met the ball anyway.

Pollock from the other end. Doing what he knows to do. Bowling fast, accurate. Ball on the middle stump. Tendulkar meets it with the full face of the bat that the bowlers have been seeing all day. It goes between the bowler and the non-striker and streaks away to the sight screen. It crashes into the metal wiring beyond long-on.

AM: Tendulkar was matching Azhar stroke for stroke at this point. While Azhar's shots bordered on the overly adventurous, Tendulkar did not look like taking a risk.

A single. Azhar is on strike. Pollock runs in again. The ball is on a length. The light willow in action this time, a flash of the blade, the ball is played on the up, dispatched in the air, past mid-on and zooming to the fence. 269/5.

AM: In one-day matches, Azhar used to announce his slog mode by summoning a separate bat at around the 40-over mark. Once that was acquired, we knew that he would go after everything. There would not be any holding back – almost like a computer game with a cheat code unlocked or a special weapon acquired.

This was a no-holds-barred stroke straight out of those ODI slog overs. He was probably in the mood too, for there is no other way to explain that hoick in the air, with a mid-on in place, off a bowler like Pollock, with the team still battling to avoid the follow-on.

The last time he had batted in Test cricket, a few days ago in the fourth innings at Durban, Azhar had holed out to wide mid-on off the same bowler while attempting the same stroke.

Adams is on, more as a clutch at available straws for the South African think-tank than as a real option. His googly is too short to make an impact. Tendulkar fetches it from outside the off and pulls it between midwicket and mid-on for four.

AM: Given his bowling action, it is a miracle that Adams did not bowl these long-hops more frequently. It is testimony to hours and hours of practice at the nets.

However, when he did bowl short from a release point that low, most batsmen could put them away without much difficulty.

The change in bowling works, although not in the way anyone could have strategised.

Azhar cuts it late, towards the left of short third man. Andrew Hudson stands there, perhaps the slowest mover among the South Africans. Azhar sprints down the wicket to what should be Tendulkar's call. He hears the 'No' a bit too late. The turn is swift and he tries to get back. But even the slowest of the South African fielders is not slow enough to allow such liberties. Hudson moves quickly to his left, puts in the dive and sends it back to Richardson. The wicket is broken.

Azhar walks back for 115, scored in six minutes short of three hours, off 110 balls, with 19 fours and a six. 280/6. The partnership is 222 in 174 minutes, in 40 overs.

This is how Laxman remembered the association:

As if to entertain Mr Mandela, Sachin and Azzu bhai put on an exhibition of batting, the likes of which I had seldom seen.

The ball flew off their bats as if pre-ordained. In the dressing room we were in a trance. Out in the stands, the fans were going berserk.

According to Dilip Vengsarkar:

The partnership was just amazing, with both of them counterattacking when so many wickets had fallen for so low a score.

Lance Klusener's version:

The way Sachin and Azhar batted in Cape Town was amazing. We always thought they would make a mistake, the ball would bounce and they were not used to the bounce in South Africa. But we were talking about two legends of Indian cricket and when they got it right there was no getting them out. We obviously had our plans but not everything goes according to plan, and when two batsmen of that calibre get going it's difficult. The way they went on and on was just amazing.

Paul Adams had this to say:

I was in the field, doing the hard work, getting the stick. But it was a treat just to watch two players of that calibre batting like that. We did have a lot of runs on the board, and could afford to enjoy the batting.

G. Viswanath, the veteran correspondent who covered the series for *The Hindu*, recalls:

A splendid counterattack. Both of them played so beautifully. After being so badly beaten in the first Test match, they made a statement that they are capable. Very few Indians would have matched it. I don't think there has been a more spectacular partnership.

AS: Azhar and Tendulkar obviously enjoyed batting together. The clashes of personality, differences of opinion – down the years a lot of it real, an equally substantial proportion the result of media speculation – did not really have an effect on their associations at the crease.

Sachin Tendulkar

Mohammad Azharuddin

'We were on the field, doing the hard work. But it was a treat just to watch two players of that calibre batting like that.' – Paul Adams

Donald, Pollock, McMillan, Klusener. Difficult to find a better pace attack. What's more, three of them could bat.

Frog in the blender
'My action was always like this.
The focus was on having fun,
bamboozling people with the turn.'
– Paul Adams

Gandhi and
his associates
in front of his
law offices in
Johannesburg

'Tell me Mr Fraser, is Don Bradman still alive?' Nelson Mandela's first question when former Australian Prime Minister Malcolm Fraser visited him in prison in 1986. Here legendary Australian actor Jack Thompson presents Mandela with a framed picture of The Don.

South Africa return to international cricket. Azhar and Clive Rice in 1991

International cricket returns to South Africa. Azhar and Kepler Wessels in 1992

Long walk to recognition: Basil D'Oliveira chaired off the ground by his Worcestershire team-mates after being selected for England

'Madiba said I should carry the shield for as long as I could.' Makhaya Ntini stands with the shield of his people during the Opening Ceremony of the 2003 World Cup

Mandela with the South African team: 2003 World Cup

Cricket fans with a portrait of Nelson Mandela during the India–South Africa Test at Johannesburg, a few days after his death, in December 2013.

A very high percentage of their partnerships ended up in significant scores. A third of them amounted to 50 or more, over a fifth into century partnerships.

Partnerships in Test cricket for India (1,500 runs, four 100-run stands)

Pair	I	R	Ave	100	50	% 100
Amarnath, Gavaskar	44	2,366	55.02	10	7	22.73%
Pujara, Vijay	45	2,813	62.51	10	9	22.22%
Azharuddin, Tendulkar	**42**	**2,385**	**58.17**	**9**	**5**	**21.43%**
Dravid, Jaffer	31	1,555	51.83	6	3	19.35%
Kohli, Rahane	53	3,271	64.13	10	14	18.87%
Chauhan, Gavaskar	60	3,127	54.85	11	10	18.33%
Sehwag, Tendulkar	23	1,560	67.82	4	5	17.39%
Dravid, Sehwag	58	3,383	60.41	10	11	17.24%
Ganguly, Tendulkar	71	4,173	61.36	12	16	16.90%
Vengsarkar, Viswanath	32	1,638	56.48	5	7	15.63%
Gavaskar, Vengsarkar	67	3,272	50.33	10	12	14.93%
Dravid, Gambhir	47	2,530	55.00	7	9	14.89%
Dravid, Ganguly	68	3,294	53.12	10	12	14.71%
Dravid, Tendulkar	143	6,920	50.51	20	29	13.99%
Dravid, Laxman	86	4,065	51.45	12	14	13.95%
Gambhir, Sehwag	87	4,412	52.52	11	25	12.64%
Laxman, Tendulkar	73	3,523	51.05	9	19	12.33%
Ganguly, Laxman	41	1,681	43.10	5	7	12.20%
Kohli, Pujara	62	2,894	47.44	7	14	11.29%
Gavaskar, Viswanath	47	1,737	37.76	4	7	8.51%
Gaekwad, Gavaskar	52	1,780	34.90	4	9	7.69%

AS: There has obviously been a number of rearguard efforts in the history of Indian cricket. Rescuing the side from desperate situations, some of them against excellent attacks as well. However, none of them was of this particular sort ... where with backs to the wall batsmen from both ends started flaying the magnificent attack with casual disdain, making a mockery of the situation, the conditions and the bowling ... and it came off in such a spectacular fashion.

In fact, the only other innings of such explosive counterattack from both ends that comes to mind was essayed in the current Twenty20 age, when K.L. Rahul and Rishabh Pant got stuck into England at The Oval during the 2018 Test series. Even in that innings the scoring rate was distinctly slower – 204 runs added in 44.3 overs.

Even those two modern batsmen nurtured on Twenty20 cricket could not quite match the rate of scoring of the earlier duo at Cape Town.

> ## *This is a good place to pause and look at some of the major rearguard partnerships in the history of Indian cricket*

AS: The first major one that comes to mind was between Lala Amarnath and C.K. Nayudu. The first ever Test match in India, a deficit of 119 and India two down for 21 in the second innings. Nichols, Clark and Verity formed a rather difficult attack for the newbies of the Test world to handle. And these two legendary Indian strokemakers added 186, Amarnath scoring the first hundred for India in Test cricket. Landmark indeed.

1933/34 vs England, Bombay Gymkhana, third wicket, Amarnath and Nayudu 186

AM: Just over two years later, Vizzy went out of his way to corner Nayudu on the England tour. He also sent Amarnath home. At Manchester, India walked out facing a deficit of 368 runs, against an attack consisting of Allen and Verity. Vizzy had tried to sabotage even at this stage, asking Mushtaq to run Merchant out. But

Mushtaq spilled the beans to Merchant, they laughed it off, and got the first two centuries for India away from home. They added 203, and the Test match was saved.
1936 vs England, Old Trafford, first wicket, Merchant and Mushtaq 203

AS: The next major rearguard partnership that comes to mind is the Hazare–Phadkar association at Adelaide. An inexperienced side against an Australian team that would soon become known as the Invincibles. Battered through the series, here they had 674 runs scored against them in the first innings, Bradman hitting 201. They were 133/5 against Lindwall, Miller, Johnson and Toshack. And then Hazare and Phadkar put on 188. It did not matter in terms of the end result, but must have been a magnificent boost for the young side. Of course, when India followed on Hazare got his second century of the match.
1947/48 vs Australia, Adelaide, sixth wicket, Hazare and Phadkar 188

AM: By now Hazare was establishing himself as among the best middle-order batsmen in the world. In the 1948/49 home series against West Indies, he found an ally in Rusi Modi. Every Test match in the series followed a pattern. Hazare and Modi had partnerships of 156, 129, 108, 64, 72 and 139 – a whopping 668 in six innings. It is difficult to pick one, but it is worth a mention that India trailed by 177, 356, 94, 337 and 93 in the five Tests and saved all but one. They could have won the last Test but for an umpiring glitch that involved miscounting balls.
1948/49 vs West Indies, Hazare and Modi, multiple

AS: India were routed by Bedser and a debutant Trueman, backed by Laker and Lock, when they toured England the following summer. The rout began in the first Test match, when India were reduced to 42/3. But Hazare still had some steam left in him. Along with his namesake, the young Manjrekar, he added 222 to rescue India, only for them to get bowled out 29 runs later.
1952 vs England, Headingley, fourth wicket, Hazare and Manjrekar 222

AM: Three losses in four Tests and India went into the fifth Test with Hemu Adhikari called up to be the fourth captain in the series. Borde scored a hundred and the new skipper 63 as India piled on 415. But the West Indian response was 644. Besides, Umrigar and Manjrekar were injured. At 135/3, Borde and Adhikari came together again, the last specialist batsmen. They added 108, saving the match. Crucial runs, since the next five batsmen managed ten runs between them. Borde missed his second hundred of the match by four runs.
1958/59 vs West Indies, Delhi, Borde and Adhikari sixth wicket 134
fourth wicket 108

AS: The 1963/64 series against England was quite a drab one, finishing 0-0 after five Tests, famous for the Nadkarni feat of 21 consecutive maidens. However, after a draw in the first Test match, India were floundering at 99/6 on the first afternoon of the second, with most of the batting back in the pavilion. The series could have been lost if that collapse had not been checked. Borde and Durani batted through the rest of the day, and remained unseparated till the middle of the first session on the second day. They added 153, and it saved the match. India continued on equal terms all through the series.

1963/64 vs England, Delhi, seventh wicket, Durani and Borde 153

AM: One of India's most famous wins came against Australia at Bombay in 1964/65. India came into the Test match 0-1 down in the three-match series, and were reduced to 122/6 in pursuit of 254. However, Pataudi, keeping in tune with his track record of bizarre batting orders, held back himself, Manjrekar, and Borde to seven, eight, and nine. He and Manjrekar added 93 in a display of utmost restraint before Borde pushed India over the finishing line.

1964/65 vs Australia, Brabourne Stadium, seventh wicket, Pataudi and Manjrekar 93

AS: The next in the list had a kind of fairy-tale whiff to it. India were getting battered as usual in Australia. Jaisimha, flown in as reinforcement, got off the plane, grabbed a battered relic of a bat, went to the middle and scored 74 in the first innings. In the second they were set 395 to win. India fought, but collapsed to 191/5. Jaisimha was joined by Borde. Two and a quarter hours later, the score was over 300 and still only five down. Lawry was a worried man.

It did not end happily, though. Borde fell at 310, and Jaisimha was the last out at 355 for 101. But it has gone down in the folklore of Indian cricket.

1967/68 vs Australia, Brisbane, sixth wicket, Jaisimha and Borde 119

AM: India's 1971 win came against one of the weaker West Indian sides, but one must keep in mind that India had never won a Test match against them, home or away, till then. While Gavaskar dominated with what still remains a record debut series aggregate of 774 runs, the stage was set when Sardesai and Solkar added 137 in the first Test after India had been reduced to 75/5. The bowling was less than ordinary, but India reached 387 from that position and forced West Indies to follow on for the first time. They did not relinquish the psychological advantage for the rest of the series.
1970/71 vs West Indies, Kingston, sixth wicket, Sardesai and Solkar 137

AS: India 96, England 419/9 declared. It cannot get any more one-sided. And in the second innings, after showing real fight, Gavaskar became Botham's 100th wicket in Test cricket. Several sessions were still left in the match. Vengsarkar and Viswanath batted together for five and a half hours to add 210 and save the Test match. Both got hundreds – it was the first of Vengsarkar's three at Lord's.
1979 vs England, Lord's, third wicket, Vengsarkar and Viswanath 210

AM: Gavaskar did not have a batting performance on English soil that would stand the test of time (the 101 on a green Old Trafford surface in 1974 got buried amidst India's dismal performance on the tour). That changed less than a month after the Viswanath–Vengsarkar stand. Facing a target of 438, he added 213 with Chauhan and 153 with Vengsarkar – two rearguard partnerships that went in vain following a curious change in batting order and England's sluggish over rate towards the end. India finished on 429/8.

1979 vs England, The Oval. First wicket, Gavaskar and Chauhan 213; second wicket, Gavaskar and Vengsarkar 155

AS: No Imran, no Sarfraz. On paper a most insipid attack. And suddenly India found themselves on 85/6 on the second morning after a rain-interrupted first day. But they batted deep those days. Binny and Madan Lal added 155, and embarrassment against the arch-rivals was avoided.

They almost did an encore against West Indies at Kanpur: 90/8 against Marshall, Holding, Davis and Baptiste, looking at a total of 494, Gavaskar's bat flung out of his hand by Marshall. Binny and Madan Lal added 117. But this time around they could not save India.

1983 vs Pakistan, Bangalore, seventh wicket, Madan Lal and Binny 155
1983 vs West Indies, Kanpur, ninth wicket, Madan Lal and Binny 117

AM: Shastri's ascent from the No. 10 slot to the top is well known. Less documented are More's many back-to-the-wall performances. He did particularly well in partnerships with Shastri (447 runs at 49.67), Vengsarkar (368 at 52.27), and Tendulkar (303 at 43.28) in addition to several stands with Kapil Dev and Prabhakar. Here, at Bridgetown, India were 63/6 after conceding a 56-run lead. Shastri and More added 133 against Marshall, Ambrose, Bishop and Walsh to help India reach 251. Their stand amounted to more than half the side's total.

1988/89 vs West Indies, Bridgetown, seventh wicket, Shastri and More 133

AS: The task was to bat out the last day. With two and a half hours to go, India collapsed to 183/6. The seasoned Prabhakar walked out to join the 17-year-old Tendulkar. The world witnessed the first of what would amount to 51 Test hundreds. Tendulkar remained unbeaten on 119. Prabhakar kept the other end secure with a typically gritty 67. When time was called India were 343/6.

1990 vs England, Old Trafford, seventh wicket, Tendulkar and Prabhakar 160*

AM: Months before the Cape Town Test match, South Africa had put up 428 at Eden Gardens and reduced India to 161/7. Then Azhar, having to retire hurt earlier in the innings, unleashed his revenge with a 77-ball 109. At the other end was Kumble, whose 88 was just as crucial in a stand that doubled India's score. The most iconic phase of the innings was when Azhar slammed five consecutive fours off the last five balls of an over from Klusener. Not to be left behind, Kumble responded with two in the first two balls of the next over, from Donald.

1996/97 vs South Africa, Kolkata, eighth wicket, Azharuddin and Kumble 161

Rearguard partnerships after the Sachin–Azhar act of 1996/97

From 82/5 to 218/5, Tendulkar and Mongia turned certain defeat to near-certain victory before the latter flat-batted Waqar down the throat of Akram at mid-on. Perhaps the greatest and saddest innings of Tendulkar's career.

1998/99 vs Pakistan, Chennai, sixth wicket, Tendulkar and Mongia 136

Two partnerships constituting what is surmised to be the watershed of Indian cricket.

Both turned the match around from being on the ropes.

The first resulted in victory after following on, the second a rare win in Australia from an almost equally hopeless position.

2000/01 vs Australia, Kolkata, fifth wicket, Laxman and Dravid 376

2003/04 vs Australia, Adelaide, fifth wicket, Dravid and Laxman 303

Usual story. First day the of tour, struggling at 68/4.

As Tendulkar started playing his shots, Sehwag, on debut, matched the master stroke for stroke.

Two superlative hundreds.

2001/02 vs South Africa, Bloemfontein, fifth wicket, Tendulkar and Sehwag 220

Lying 260 runs behind and on the brink of going down 0-2 in the three-Test series, the score read 11/2 when Flintoff dismissed Jaffer.

Dravid and Tendulkar batted together for the rest of the fourth day and much of the fifth morning.

2002 vs England, Trent Bridge, third wicket, Dravid and Tendulkar 163

On the fourth afternoon, the last six Indian wickets required another 52 to make West Indies bat again.

Tendulkar took charge, adding 214 with – who else this being Eden? – Laxman to save the Test match.

2002/03 vs West Indies, Kolkata, fifth wicket, Tendulkar and Laxman 214

Laxman and Dhoni have added 1,361 runs in 24 innings at 56.70. Put in a 750-run cut-off, and neither has had a better average with any of their partners.

Here they took India from 93/5 to the safety of 276, securing a 45-run lead which turned out to be match-winning.

2007/08 vs Pakistan, Delhi, sixth wicket, Laxman and Dhoni 183

Needing 216 to win, India collapsed to 124/8.

A limping Laxman stood at one end and the gangly form of Ishant at the other.

They added 81 in an eventual one-wicket win.

2010/11 vs Australia, Mohali, ninth wicket, Laxman and Ishant 81

India were 57/2 after being set 364 to win against Johnson, Harris, Siddle and Lyon on a deteriorating Adelaide pitch.

Vijay and Kohli added 185 at a shade under four an over. India glorious in defeat and Kohli regal.

2014/15 vs Australia, Adelaide, third wicket, Vijay and Kohli 185

Two batsmen criticised through the tour came together at 121/5, the target 464. They launched a counterattack

from both ends that comes closest to the Tendulkar–
Azhar show at Cape Town.

By tea on the final afternoon, the possibility of
victory was not too much of a stretch. India finally
fell, but on their sword.

2018 vs England, The Oval, sixth wicket, Rahul and
Pant 204

AS: Azhar remained an enigma. I remember watching
cricket through most of the 1990s, among fellow students
in a television lounge, or in the crowd at Eden Gardens,
or in a crowded canteen or restaurant where people had
taken a hasty break to catch a few moments of the match.
From 1995 onwards, there would be one lapse of Azhar,
a dismissal or a fumble or the rare dropped catch … and
comments would fly around, 'Azhar is finished.'

And yet, he kept resurrecting himself, again and again,
with some unbelievable innings. He remained the fittest
in the side.

People had written him off after his failure in the World
Cup, in England, after the loss of the captaincy. And then
from the Eden Test match onwards he enjoyed some of the
best days of his career. Three more years, 27 more Tests,
close to another 2,000 runs, eight hundreds, and another
stint as captain. Even in his final Test innings, he made a
hundred, an impeccable one with none of the others getting
more than 26. Once again the opponents were South Africa.

AM: Azhar's last Test match is forgotten amidst the
unfortunate chain of events that emerged in 2000. Battered
and bruised after a 0-3 whitewash in Australia, India were
swept away 0-2 by South Africa at home. This was the
first time they had lost a series at home since 1986/87,

and remains the only time they have been whitewashed in a series of two Tests or more on Indian soil.

Starting the innings 321 in arrears, India were 71/3 when Azhar walked out. He scored 102 of the 169 India managed during his stay, dominating a bowling attack on a pitch that had troubled every other Indian batsman.

The batting was as fluent, the fitness as unyielding, and he seemed to have shed five years with the moustache. He seemed good enough for a few more years.

That was not to happen. The man with a highest score of 199 ended his career with 99 Test matches.

Unfortunate? Perhaps. But then, had Raman Lamba not picked up a last-minute injury ahead of the Karachi Test match of 1989/90, Azhar's career might have faced a setback, his appointment as captain would definitely have been delayed, and he would have played fewer Tests. That injury went on to alter the course of Indian cricket in the 1990s.

Things perhaps balanced out in the end.

Tendulkar's greatness is easier to demonstrate. The numbers do the work. If they need more, there are many, many quotes from colleagues, adversaries, writers, the entire cricket fraternity.

It is different with Azhar. His fans will be the first to point out that his career record features obvious weaknesses. No coach is likely to ask their wards to imitate him.

If you look at his batting on YouTube, you will find his strokeplay breathtaking, but he was not the first batsman to earn that tag, and nor will he be the last.

It is not about fielding either. True, Azhar had his distinctive pick-up and throw (invariably accurate) from behind his legs. He took absurd catches in the slip cordon. He ran faster than almost any of his team-mates. He was one of the greatest all-round fielders of all time.

And while he had converted India into an invincible unit at home, they failed to win a single Test under him outside Asia.

But Azharisms were not restricted to batting and fielding alone.

How do you explain his enigmatic image? Consider that Titan Cup match at Bangalore months before this Test match, when crowd disturbance held up play.

Azhar was out of form. He had been involved in a showdown with Sidhu in England. He had been recently sacked as captain. His personal life was being dissected by the media and discussed around the nation. News of his rifts with Tendulkar had been doing the rounds.

Yet, he stepped out to calm the crowd. It worked.

A cult hero.

Afternoon Light

Mongia is the new man in. Supposedly he thinks like a batsman, but he will end with a Test average of 24, even lower than Kirmani and More who were combative lower-order men with no claims of being genuine batters. But then, he has scored a Test hundred as an opening batsman not too long ago.

AS: That 152 by Mongia. I used to work as a quantitative process analyst in the late 1990s, and this innings was the example I often used when explaining that the best performance is not really proof of ability. It can often be an outlier. For someone who gave every indication that he knew how to build an innings and often batted as high as No. 3 for his state side, Mongia ended with a career batting average of 24, less than More, less than Kirmani … much less than what one expected of him.

AM: And while we are on batting of wicketkeepers, several Indian stumpers between More and Dhoni impressed with the bat. Mongia, Ajay Ratra, Deep Dasgupta and Dinesh Karthik all got Test hundreds, while Parthiv Patel's return to the Test side after a decade's hiatus was as an opener.

Promoting the wicketkeeper to the top is not a recent practice for India. Of the 36 men who have kept wicket for them in Test cricket, 14 have opened the batting.

The trend began in 1932, when Janardan Navle faced the first ball for India in Test cricket. Navle opened for India in their first two Test matches, Dilawar Hussain in the next two, and Dattaram Hindlekar in the one after that. Then Vijay Merchant and Mushtaq Ali established themselves as a pair.

AS: While still on the batting prowess of Indian wicketkeepers, Dighe was instrumental in winning that cliffhanger of a Test match at Chennai to clinch the series against Australia in 2001. His runs in the final moments were crucial.

AM: That is one of the best fourth-innings performances by a Test debutant. In the post-Dhoni era, Saha, apart from being the best Indian gloveman in the televised era, has also impressed with the bat, even overseas. And while Pant's wicketkeeping has been criticised, his hundred in England and an excellent series in Australia have made him a genuine candidate for the slot of a specialist batsman.

Adams pitches short again, this time the regular ball that comes in to the right-hander. Tendulkar pulls again, but square. There are men on the leg side but no one anywhere near the path of the ball. 289/6. The first target is 41 runs away.

AS: Those were the fierce pulls Tendulkar used to essay through most of the 1990s. Towards the end of the decade he had that accident which led to lower back problems. Following that, we used to see him prefer to sway back and play the uppercut over the slips. He continued to play the pull, but only to deliveries that were on his body. If there was even a bit of room towards his off side, he would prefer the uppercut.

AM: Tendulkar used the uppercut abundantly during his 155 at Bloemfontein in 2001/02. He can be credited for bringing it back among Indians.

For India, Mushtaq Ali was one of the earliest exponents of the shot, but the Indian slow, low pitches in the decades that followed – often designed to assist spinners – were hardly ideal for subsequent attempts.

The following ball is tossed up. Tendulkar meets it on the full. It is easy meat. The silly point leaps up and turns. The extra cover area is scorched yet again. The thud on the boundary board is the constant background accompaniment to the batsmanship in the middle. 293/6.

AS: One of the features of Tendulkar in full flow was his seamless adjustment to changes of pace. Pace from one end and spin from the other, he would play almost the same strokes, put them away to the same corners of the ground, the adjustment for the type of bowling too subtle and built into his fluency to be visible to the mortal naked eye.

AM: Lara was the only other batsman in the 1990s and early 2000s who could switch so effortlessly against the same challenges. It was never easy to take on Vaas and Murali in Sri Lanka with little support at the other end.

Adams strikes. Mongia fails to negotiate a straighter one and is rapped on the pads. The appeal splits the air, the finger goes up, Adam flips himself through the air, the South African physio, medic and management go through their usual palpitations of anxiety. Mongia walks back for 5. 298/7. There are still 32 runs to get to make the hosts bat again.

AS: The tail was in, but with Kumble and Srinath it was quite a decent one. And Tendulkar did have a few good partnerships with the tail over his career.

AM: Tendulkar's associations with tail-enders started with the Napier Test match of 1989/90, when he added 128 with Kiran More to rescue India. Two years later he added 81 at Perth, once again with More, against a superior bowling attack. There were several after that.

Tendulkar's notable partnerships with late-order batsmen (partnerships with established batsmen and all-rounders excluded)

W	R Partner	vs	Venue	Season
10th	133 Zaheer Khan	Bangladesh	Dhaka	2004/05
9th	81 Kiran More	Australia	Perth	1991/92
8th	129 Harbhajan Singh	Australia	Sydney	2007/08
7th	128 Kiran More	New Zealand	Napier	1989/90
7th	76 Harbhajan Singh	South Africa	Cape Town	2010/11
7th	58 Anil Kumble	England	Edgbaston	1996
7th	52 Harbhajan Singh	England	Trent Bridge	2011
4th	144 Amit Mishra*	England	The Oval	2011

*Mishra was a nightwatchman

Cronje comes on to bowl a few tight overs to rest the fast bowlers for the new ball. For some reason Tendulkar is habitually hesitant against the South African captain. He has no issues facing the thunderbolts of Donald and Pollock. However, whenever Cronje comes on with his gentle medium pace, the great bat struts around in some confusion.

But Cronje finally errs, dropping it short. Tendulkar pulls it round the corner for four.

AS: For some reason, loose balls such as these bowled by irregular bowlers while Tendulkar was in full flow always worried me. Cronje dismissed him in both innings in the third Test of this series. And then there were Mark Waugh at Wankhede in 2001 and Michael Vaughan at Trent Bridge in 2002.

AM: Back in 1992/93, Tendulkar had become Cronje's first wicket in Test cricket, and later his third. Cronje would dismiss Tendulkar five times in 11 Tests. After his retirement, Tendulkar revealed how he hated facing his South African counterpart. When Cronje came on to bowl to him – on more than one occasion – Tendulkar would ask him, 'Why don't you give me Allan Donald?'

Cronje would finish with 43 Test wickets at 29.95, an average better than perceived. Tendulkar featured four times in his first 13 wickets.

One curious aspect of his bowling career was his performance against the subcontinent teams.

Hansie Cronje's bowling statistics, by opposition

Opposition	M	W	Ave		M	W	Ave
India	11	14	22.57		22	24	21.50
Pakistan	6	4	25.50		(Subcontinent teams)		
Sri Lanka	5	6	16.33				
Australia	12	5	49.40		43	15	49.00
England	18	3	86.33		(Others barring Zimbabwe)		
New Zealand	7	4	44.00				
West Indies	6	3	17.67				
Zimbabwe	3	4	9.25				
Career	**68**	**43**	**29.95**				

AS: Cronje had a superb economy rate of 2.03 through his career. He was difficult to get away, making him a perfect foil for the excellent South African attacks. Perhaps due to the usual firepower of the front-line South African bowling attacks he was considered the weak link and batsmen tried to relax a bit against him or take liberties. Besides, his pace worked on the sluggish subcontinent wickets, making him very difficult to get away.

Cronje pitches up this time and once again there is that broad bat meeting the ball with full face and the red streak flashing across the turf behind the bowler to the bottom of the sight screen. Yet another superlative straight drive. 309/7.

AS: Tendulkar might have been somewhat apprehensive against Cronje, but you could not get away with overpitching when he was in that sort of form. Sublime timing and he did away with the necessity of the follow-through yet again.

The ability versus best-effort argument bears out yet again. Kumble cannot counter Donald here as he did a few weeks earlier at the Eden Gardens. A touch to Richardson and it is 315/8. Still 15 runs to get to save the follow-on. In walks Javagal Srinath.

AS: There had been that home series against West Indies in 1993/94 when Srinath had scored 136 runs at 45.33 with two fifties, one of them a match-winning 60. When he was batting with the Indian No. 11 Venkatapathy Raju at Mohali in the first innings of the third Test match, the West Indian bowlers were happy to give him a single and attack Raju. He scored another half-century on that difficult Birmingham wicket in the first Test match of the 1996 summer. He averaged in the early 20s at that time, good enough to qualify as a bowling all-rounder. In fact, at Johannesburg in the third Test of this series he would get 41 in the first innings. Not a bad man to come in at No. 10.

But somehow down the way he lost his ability to bat. A couple of blows to the fingers did not help. He did not get behind the ball any more, trying instead to move away and cart balls through the off side. Earlier he used to pull fast bowlers off his body. He ended with an average of 14.21, including 9 in his last 26 Tests.

AM: Till 1995, Srinath averaged 22.54 with the bat, compared to Kumble's 14.27. Following that their batting careers followed opposite tracks. By the time he retired (he reached the 1,000-run mark in his last Test match), Srinath's average had dropped to 14.21. Kumble finished with 17.77.

AS: Of course, for all the bucketloads of wickets Kumble took, one of his happiest memories would remain the century at The Oval in 2007.

New ball taken. At 4:40 in the afternoon, Donald steams in. Not a half-volley, not really room to free his arms. Yet Tendulkar takes a step forward and crashes it through extra cover with extreme audacity. The Indian captain raises his bat. 153 in 306 minutes, 238 balls, studded with 23 fours. The follow-on is averted.

AS: These two innings were both fit for the most discerning gods of cricket. However, if I am asked to pick one stroke among the 45 boundaries and one six struck by the two men this would be it. Donald charging in with the new ball, on a good length, not much room, nothing wrong with the ball, and Tendulkar cracking it through the covers, hitting it on the up.

AM: For me, it would be Azhar's pull off Donald. Probably not his best of the day but the sheer arrogance defined the zone he was in.

Pollock knocks back Srinath's stumps. 340/9.

AS: Srinath played a pretty decent innings in the circumstances, sticking around for 36 minutes and helping Tendulkar take the side past the follow-on mark. As we discussed, Srinath was a pretty stubborn batsman in those days. In ODIs, he was sent in as a pinch hitter.

AM: He even hit a fifty against the South Africans at Rajkot during the 1996 tour, batting at No. 3 and actually building his innings and taking 69 balls over his 53.

Dodda Ganesh is in to bat. The No. 11 on debut. Having bowled 23.5 overs, no wicket for 93.

AS: Not a bad batsman actually. He ended with over 2,000 first-class runs at 18.39 with a hundred in the Ranji Trophy against Vidarbha. In the previous season he had scored 75 against Hyderabad. I am sure the Indian team knew about his batting abilities. For example, in that match against Hyderabad, Dravid had played alongside him for Karnataka, and Laxman was one of the members of the Hyderabad side.

AM: However, I don't think Tendulkar was really counting on him.

Pollock runs in. The last bit of restraint has departed from Tendulkar with Ganesh at the other end. He throws his bat into a magnificent cover drive. The sweeper sprints across but cannot get around in time. 345/9.

AS: It is difficult to pinpoint one feature of Tendulkar's strokeplay that stood out. The straight drive is perhaps most celebrated because it seems so pure when one looks at it. But be it the fierce pulls, the later-day uppercuts or the cheeky paddle sweeps, each stroke carried the Tendulkar signature. Similarly, the cover drive carried its own majesty. There is something inherently classy about drives through the off side. The entire concept about flourishing batting of the Golden Age of Cricket was based on that. And the confidence and audacity with which Tendulkar played it in his prime was extraordinary.

However, considering the highly productive nature of the stroke, it was quite a surreal experience to see him eschew it totally for the 241 not out at Sydney, 2003/04, because he had been caught flashing outside the off stump

181

a few times. An insight into the adaptability that allowed him to play for so many years at the very top of his game. The second peak from 2007 to 2011 was quite unbelievable. Much of it had to do with the way he had adapted his style to suit the erosion of time.

Dodda Ganesh's bat is all over the place, in all manners of anachronism, groping for the ball in distant areas weeks after it has reached the wicketkeeper. Yet, he does not get a touch. Perhaps he is not a decent enough batsman to do so. And the ball does not hit the wicket. Donald cannot believe it. He stares at the bowler from Karnataka and lets forth a torrent of colourful epithets. As he walks back Tendulkar tells him that Ganesh does not speak Hindi, let alone English. If he wants his words to get through, he must abuse him in Kannada.

AS: That is perhaps one tactic that no side has ever experimented with. To break down the fast bowling terrors. A stonewalling No. 11 without a common language is bound to drive the most terrifying fast bowler up the wall.

AM: Now in 2020, Ganesh is quite articulate in English. When I spoke to him about the match, he told me he picked up English while playing in England.

Frustration is writ large on Donald's face as he pitches short. Tendulkar is on to it in a flash, pulling it with a crack like a rifle shot, and the eye can scarcely keep pace as it thuds against the boards in front of square. 350 up. Tendulkar has 100 in boundaries.

AS: In attacking mood, Tendulkar of the 1990s took on the short balls of the fastest bowlers spontaneously. It was quite an exhilarating sight.

He did pull fiercely later in his career, but not as frequently. One instance of his throwing everything at the bowling at a later date was glimpsed at Headingley in 2002. Three sixes in that innings. One off Alex Tudor was pulled straight into the brickwork beyond square leg. Another off Andy Caddick pulled over square leg almost with a straight bat. The third was off Matthew Hoggard, but that was not really something common in a Test match. Fast bowler steaming in, near-dark conditions, Tendulkar taking a couple of steps down the wicket and cross-batting a length ball over widish long-on. He made 193 in that knock.

AM: However, his most-remembered six off a short ball came in the World Cup the next year, off Caddick. There was no issue with the light that day, but what stood out was the distance it travelled.

Yet another bouncer. Yet another swivel. Yet another instance of the bat sending the ball screaming to the square-leg fence. Donald cannot take it anymore. He lets go at Tendulkar. The little man ignores him. Ganesh looks amused.

AS: Generally, as Tendulkar got older, he kept his pulls down on the ground in Test matches. He stuck to taking the aerial route with pulls only in ODIs. The uppercut and the straight boundaries were more six-hitting zones in Test matches. He hooked a six off Morkel to get to his final Test hundred, his 51st, on this very ground 14 years later. An exceptional innings. But that six came off the top edge and went over the wicketkeeper.

He adapted his game as he aged. That was the secret of his continuing at the top for so long. His strike rate remained more or less the same down the years. He waited for the ball, did not play on the up as much as he used to. He managed to get his runs at the same rate using less head-on methods. However, around the world the rate of scoring in Test matches generally went up. So, we can probably say that he became a slightly slower batsman in terms of how the world changed.

AM: Despite slowing down, Tendulkar finished with a strike rate of 54, which is decent.

AS: When Tendulkar retired Dennis Amiss told me in an interview, 'In the early days he was marvellous at coming forward. He didn't get pushed back by the faster bowlers in Test match cricket. Down the years, he probably did not come at the ball quite so much, especially early on in the innings. He stayed back in his crease a bit more, and waited and watched.'

Brian McMillan from round the wicket. Angling the short delivery outside the off stump. Tendulkar pulls, gets it well over Adam Bacher at deep backward square. The young man runs back, jumps, falls back, tumbles and somehow holds it in his outstretched right hand and keeps holding it as he hits the ground.

Paul Adams remembers: 'It took a rather special catch by Adam Bacher to get rid of Tendulkar. He had pulled the short ball, and he ran back, jumped and held on to it as he fell.'

Tendulkar looks on in disbelief. 169 from 254 balls in just under five and a half hours. 26 boundaries. India all out for 359.

AS: It looked six. Donald said so in his autobiography as well. And Adam Bacher plucked it out of thin air.

Years later Dilip Vengsarkar told me, 'The knock Sachin played there was extraordinary. It was a true Viv Richards-style innings, dominating Donald, Pollock and everyone else. He was at his peak at that time. Towards the end of the day Sachin got out … I remember [Adam Bacher] catching him one-handed in front of the boundary … It was a great innings.'

AM: Adam Bacher was a member of the gold-medal-winning South African cricket sides at the 2005 and 2009 Maccabiah Games. But his name will forever evoke memories of this catch more than anything else.

AS: Adam Bacher. The nephew of the famous Ali Bacher. One Indian journalist, rather unprepared, asked Dr Ali Bacher how he felt about his son playing for South Africa. The good doctor answered, 'When he plays well, he's my son. Else he's my nephew.'

Dr Bacher was undoubtedly impressed. 'The most extraordinary thing happened, my nephew caught him spectacularly in the deep,' he told G. Viswanath 20 years after the catch.

Ali Bacher

Almost every move of captain Bacher came off in the 1970 series against Australia. South Africa triumphed 4-0.

Eric Rowan was convinced even before the series that he was a hell of a good captain.

After the final Test match, Ali Bacher was chaired off the ground.

Modestly, Bacher himself suggested that the 1970 side was so great that a captain was redundant.

When the future of the 1970 tour of England hung in balance Bacher's statements remained guarded. He said that he would welcome multiracial cricket as soon as it was considered practical by the government. He discussed with Springbok rugby captain Dawie de Villiers about what to expect in England. While stating that he would love to speak to a demonstrator provided the latter was polite, Bacher insisted that they should not be allowed to break up a tour.

SACHIN AND AZHAR AT CAPE TOWN

For a man who would later work tirelessly to keep cricket alive and fair in South Africa during and after the isolation years, his statement included that perennial cliché: 'We are not politicians, we are going to England to play cricket.'

However, he did publicly defend the right of protesters to stage peaceful demonstrations.

All the while he was working as a medical doctor in a hospital for non-Europeans near Johannesburg. It was not really that easy to speak against prevalent government policies in South Africa in those days.

During the years of isolation, Bacher worked furiously to level the playing field. To ensure that the standard of cricket was maintained in the land, to ensure that rebel cricketers were lured to tour and play against the best of the country. He also tried to ensure that South Africa re-emerged in the international scene in a manner acceptable to the world.

Bacher was also one of the earliest to recognise that South African cricket would have to embrace the non-white cricketers and communities if they were to have a realistic chance of returning to the big league. He pioneered mass coaching clinics and development programmes in the black townships.

By 1990 signs and symptoms hinted at the end of the bleak era, and Bacher had the foresight to form a single colour-independent body to oversee all cricket in South Africa. To this end, he worked in close collaboration with Steve Tshwete, the head of the sports desk of the African National Congress. This was followed by Bacher and Tshwete's triumphant London visit, which saw South Africa's re-admission into the ICC.

186

Bacher was the manager of the Clive Rice-led South African team which embarked on the historic tour to India in 1991. Through the next 12 years, he reigned as the most influential figure in South African cricket.

There were hiccups, major ones. His goal was such that he could not please all.

His drive to organise rebel tours has led critics to ask questions about his ethics. And later there have been issues with the World Cup funds.

He has also been associated with the evils of reverse-apartheid in South African cricket. Kevin Pietersen has gone on record saying that it was Bacher's rudeness and stubborn adherence to the quota system that led him to leave South Africa and ply his trade in England.

And then in April 2000 he was suddenly woken up in the wee hours by a sobbing Hansie Cronje.

Besides, in 2003 other avenues had opened up for cricketers who felt discriminated against because of the quota: Kolpak.

But, Bacher was a key player in resuming normal sport in a society that stuttered and stumbled back towards some kind of normality.

Tendulkar out for 169. In the press box Dilip Vengsarkar sighs: 'If he had some support from the others, he could get that 200.'

AS: That 200 remained elusive till 1999. There were many theories. Gavaskar voiced something about his forearms tiring after reaching 160. Indeed, he had got out between 160 and 179 five times before 1999.

And suddenly in the next five years he had five doubles and several other huge hundreds.

Tendulkar's high scores, 1989–1999	Tendulkar's high scores, 1999–2004
165 vs Eng, Chennai, 1992/93	217 vs NZ, Ahmedabad, 1999/00
179 vs WI, Nagpur, 1994/95	201* vs Zim, Nagpur, 2000/01
177 vs Eng, Nottingham, 1996	155 vs SA, Bloemfontein, 2001/02
169 vs SA, Cape Town, 1996/97	176 vs Zimbabwe, Nagpur, 2001/02
155* vs Aus, Chennai, 1997/98	193 vs Eng, Headingley, 2002
177 vs Aus, Bangalore, 1997/98	176 vs WI, Kolkata, 2002/03
	241* vs Aus, Sydney, 2003/04
	194* vs Pak, Multan, 2003/04

AS: Similarly, 236 not out by Gavaskar remained the highest individual score for India for 18 years. Gavaskar himself was embarrassed by it. According to him a country which had been playing Test cricket since 1932 should have had a much bigger score as the record.

Before Gavaskar, Vinoo Mankad's 231 had stood as the Indian record for 28 years.

AM: By 1994/95, India were the only Test-playing nation without an individual score of 250. Dave Houghton scored 266 against Sri Lanka, a run short of Aravinda de Silva's 267 not out earlier that decade. Sanath Jayasuriya got Sri Lanka's first triple-hundred in 1997.

Glenn Turner had scored 259 in West Indies back in 1972. Both Martin Crowe (299) and Bryan Young (267*) crossed the 250-run mark in the 1990s.

And for South Africa, Jackie McGlew had crossed the 250-run barrier in 1952/53 – before even the first Indian double-hundred.

AS: Laxman went past Gavaskar in 2001. It broke a dam of sorts. In the next three and a half years we had Tendulkar 241*, Sehwag 309, Dravid 270, Tendulkar 248. Since

2001 Gavaskar's score has been overhauled 13 times in the next 19 years.

AM: Sehwag's arrival played a role in this. For some time he held the top *three* scores for India. Barring Bradman, he is the only batsman in history to cross 280 thrice in Test cricket.

Shortly after that 281, Laxman sat down next to Sehwag at a team dinner during the ODI series against Australia that followed. At that point Sehwag was yet to play Test cricket, but he was certainly not low on confidence, telling VVS: 'I know you made 281 in Kolkata, and it was a special knock. You missed a triple-century. You should have gone on to make a 300. But I know I will make a triple-hundred for India in Test cricket.'

Sehwag got that triple-hundred in three years' time, then broke his own record, and got a 293 – all in the same decade.

He was not merely synonymous with quick scoring. He redefined the term.

AS: Some say there used to be a mental block around 236. My own hypothesis is that the recent spurt of high scores also has something to do with an increased awareness of fitness matters. The batsmen got fitter down the years, and were able to play long Test innings without getting bogged down by fatigue and thereby losing concentration.

If you remember till the late 1980s and even into the 1990s the Indian cricketers used to drink the aerated beverages of their sponsors from the drinks trolley during the international matches. Cola and other aerated drinks, which are not really the healthiest stuff.

By the early 2000s, Dravid was sending his sweat samples to be analysed to get special custom-made sports drinks prepared and delivered, which would replace the key ingredients he was losing due to perspiration.

So, increased high scores in my opinion had a lot to do with increased fitness through awareness. Down the line we got the sculpted athletes like the Kohlis of today.

And of course, in the case of Sehwag, the rate of scoring had a lot to do with it.

AM: Sehwag was an aberration. His footwork, or lack thereof, did make puritans cringe – I would say some even wanted him to fail.

AS: That's common enough when people try to hang on to their worldview in face of counter-intuitive evidence.

AM: On one occasion, the usually calm John Wright grabbed him by the collar and demanded an explanation after Sehwag threw his wicket away. But then, as Wright himself admitted, Sehwag had a very still head, which was one of the crucial reasons behind his success.

The mindset, of course, was what set him apart. Ganguly once mentioned how restless Sehwag used to be in the dressing room when a team-mate, even someone as aggressive as Tendulkar, was at the crease. Every now and then Sehwag would let out an exasperated cry, for a ball defended was a boundary opportunity lost.

236 and beyond

Sunil Gavaskar	236*	West Indies	Chennai	1983/84
VVS Laxman	281	Australia	Kolkata	2000/01
Sachin Tendulkar	241*	Australia	Sydney	2003/04
Virender Sehwag	309	Pakistan	Multan	2003/04
Rahul Dravid	270	Pakistan	Rawalpindi	2003/04
Sachin Tendulkar	248*	Bangladesh	Dhaka	2004/05
Virender Sehwag	254	Pakistan	Lahore	2005/06
Sourav Ganguly	239	Pakistan	Bengaluru	2007/08
Virender Sehwag	319	South Africa	Chennai	2008/09

Virender Sehwag	293	Sri Lanka	Brabourne	2009/10
Karun Nair	303*	England	Chennai	2016/17
Virat Kohli	243	Sri Lanka	Delhi	2017/18
Virat Kohli	254*	South Africa	Pune	2019/20
Mayank Agarwal	243	Bangladesh	Indore	2019/20

End Note:

B. Sreeram points out that the two days of 4 and 5 January 1997 were made in the heaven of aesthetic batting.

The five most beautiful batsmen to watch at the time were perhaps, in no particular order, Tendulkar, Azhar, Lara, Mark Waugh and Carl Hooper.

On 4 January Tendulkar and Azhar played these two masterpieces at Cape Town.

On the following day, 5 January, Australia played West Indies at Brisbane in the Carlton & United Three-Nation ODI series. Mark Waugh cruised to 102 in Australia's score of 281/4. In response, West Indies got the runs with seven balls to spare, Lara creaming 102 and Hooper remaining unbeaten with a run-a-ball 110. The two added 154 in another exhilarating association in the shorter format of the game.

At the End of the Day

The match continues. Prasad is injured, so Dodda Ganesh takes the new ball with Srinath and dismisses Kirsten for a duck.

AM: Ganesh was debuting in that Test match. He was replacing his Karnataka team-mate David Johnson. Along with Srinath, Prasad and Kumble, they formed an all-Karnataka bowling attack.

> Sunil Joshi of Karnataka had made his debut the previous year, at Edgbaston, presumably as a *batting* all-rounder. He had not got a bowl, though he batted at six. Srinath, Prasad and Kumble all played in that Test match.
>
> When Joshi returned for the Delhi Test match against Australia, he joined Prasad, Kumble and a debutant Johnson to form a Karnataka quartet.
>
> It is not common for four *bowlers* from one domestic team to play in the same Test match. It is even rarer for a country like India, where there are so many teams.
>
> Subhash Gupte, Vinoo Mankad, Dattu Phadkar, Buck Divecha and G.S. Ramchand – all Bombay cricketers – had played for India in different combinations of four in the 1950s.

All five played at Madras during the fourth Test match of the 1952/53 series against Pakistan. Their Bombay team-mate Polly Umrigar, who often bowled, also played, but did not roll his arm over in Pakistan's only innings.

AM: In an interview, Ganesh told me that it had always been his dream to open the bowling for India in a Test match with Srinath. Now, with Prasad injured, that dream was fulfilled. Trapping Kirsten for a duck with a ball that straightened was quite an icing.

Things look even better when Srinath traps Bacher leg before, also for a duck. South Africa 7/2, the lead 177.

But, like most things cricket, the Test match does not have a fairy-tale ending. Cullinan 55, Hudson 55, South Africa declare at 256/6, a target of 427. The only way India will achieve it is if there is another miraculous association like the one in the first innings.

Like lightning strikes, it is not an easily repeatable affair. Only Laxman impresses, batting two and a quarter hours for an unbeaten 35. The rest fall away like flies.

It ends when Prasad jumps out to slog Adams. Dave Richardson whips off the bails with relish. In 33 Test matches he has 119 catches, but this is his first stumping. In his penultimate Test match he will stump Greg Blewett off Pat Symcox. Only two stumpings in a 42-Test career alongside 150 catches.

AS: It was special enough for Paul Adams to still recall it. 'I remember getting Dave Richardson his first stumping in Test cricket, when I dismissed Venkatesh Prasad.'

AM: Of all the wicketkeepers with more than 100 dismissals, no one has as few stumpings as Richardson.

It underlines the South African dependence on pace during his days.

AS: This decided the series. As captain Tendulkar had won the one-off Test match against Australia, and that keenly contested series at home against South Africa. This loss was the start of the downturn of his captaincy graph. It went downhill pretty soon.

AM: I have always felt Tendulkar got a raw deal as captain. He started with a Test match against Australia. While they did not have Warne, McGrath was there. And even if we ignore that Test match against Australia, he led India in six Tests against South Africa, three at home, three away. As we have seen, South Africa were the strongest team of the decade.

AS: A fair result should have been 2-1 for South Africa in this series. Which would have been quite a balanced outcome of the two series against that strong South African outfit. Going to South Africa, the most difficult opposition in that era, without a third seamer of note, is not easy.

AM: The lack of a third seamer hurt Tendulkar on this tour. He did have a world-class spinner in Kumble, but he did not quite live up to expectations. Had Kumble repeated his Johannesburg 1992 feat at the same venue this time, India would have got their first win on South African soil.

One cannot help but think what might have happened had Prabhakar been recalled for the England and South Africa tours.

AS: Richie Benaud said, captaincy is 90% luck and 10% skill … but, for heaven's sake, don't try it without that little 10%.

Of course, there is a danger associated with attaching axiomatic properties to such aphorisms. As our good friend

Kartikeya Date writes, 'If we consider realistic candidates for modern Test captaincy (as opposed to the era of the amateur when social class played a big role in determining who could be considered for the job) – modern Test players who are established in the first XI – how likely is it that any one of them will not possess that 10% skill?' I tend to agree with him and consider captaincy an overrated feature of the game.

However, it is true that a huge percentage of success as captain depends on luck. And the team you get constitutes much of the luck. If, for instance, as a captain you have Roberts, Holding, Garner and Marshall bowling for you, or McGrath and Warne bowling with Hayden, Langer and Ponting batting and Gilchrist after them, you don't need to do much other than turn up and win matches.

However, when India went to West Indies almost immediately after this, they were without Srinath who had broken down after the South African tour. Prasad and Abey Kuruvilla took the new ball. To try and compete with that attack in West Indies is near futile. Still they came close to winning the series, and would have done it had they not been 81 all out trying to get 120 for a win at Barbados.

AM: There are two ways to look at that 81 all out. While one cannot help but admit that the batsmen had failed, a pace attack better than Prasad, Kuruvilla and Ganesh would have made a difference – especially after India led by 21. West Indies had Bishop, Ambrose, Rose and Dillon: there was no comparison.

AS: The lack of firepower was evident when Rose and Dillon added 33 for the last wicket after being 107/9. It virtually turned the match on its head. One express bowler firing in straight could have won it for India that day. And after that, having taken the lead, West Indies shut up shop, playing dull, boring draws on placid wickets.

And when India came back, it was yet another overseas assignment to Sri Lanka on the most placid track since The Oval 1938.

AM: Add to that the fact that the Tendulkar era took off with three new middle-order batsmen, one of whom had to be accommodated at the top.

It is curious, the way the team of 2000 and beyond is often cited as a 'new era'. The team had several cricketers who had been around for at least four years at the highest level.

AS: Yes, the team of 2000 actually cut their teeth under Tendulkar and Azhar and by the time Ganguly had taken over, they had all established themselves in the side. Sehwag was the only one among the group who came after that among the batsmen.

AM: Tendulkar's baptism was, in a way, similar to Azhar's (though probably not as difficult), who had to lead in New Zealand, England, Australia and South Africa before getting a second Test match at home as captain.

AS: Tendulkar's second stint as captain was rather terrible. However, again, he was pitted against the two strongest opponents. He did okay against the New Zealanders at home, won the series in spite of that faux pas of enforcing the follow-on and then reversing the decision. But then it was against Australia Down Under with a team that was far from settled. Yes, Laxman did hit that 167 in the final Test match, a largely inconsequential innings when the match was all but over.

Those two Tendulkar solos at Melbourne truly underlined how one-dimensional the side was. Then it ᴴ## AT THE END OF THE DAY

was South Africa at home, yet again, the best travelling side of that era.

AM: While South Africa were a strong side, India should have done better than a 0-2 result on home soil. Of course, all the furore surrounding match-fixing controversies almost certainly contributed to that.

AS: Yes, in the first Test match they did manage to take the first innings lead. Largely through another incredible Tendulkar solo: 97 and 3-10, clinching a 49-run lead even after being bowled out for 225. But they fell away after that.

Perhaps the moments of triumph for Tendulkar the captain, apart from his inaugural Test match at the helm and the home series against South Africa, was the Titan Cup. But that was a hit and miss affair, with South Africa winning everything in front of them before choking in the final.

AM: Then there was the Sahara Cup. No Srinath, no Prasad, no Kumble. Pakistan had won the series the year before. But Ganguly produced the greatest all-round series performance between Greg Chappell in 1980/81 and Lance Klusener in the 1999 World Cup, and India won 4-1 after losing the first match.

AS: But the Sahara Cup was, after all, a bilateral series, and Titan Cup a three-nation tournament. So, even if we take them into account, we cannot really count too many major achievements during Tendulkar's captaincy. In the end, he led in 25 Test matches, won four and lost nine. Eight of those Tests were against South Africa, four against Australia, five against West Indies in their backyard when they were still a very decent side.

We can perhaps say Tendulkar the captain was hard done by, more so because he never got to lead against

197

a minnow. Now consider the first series after he was replaced at the helm. India played Bangladesh in the latter's inaugural Test match followed by a home series against Zimbabwe.

AM: In fact, after that Bangladesh Test match, India and Zimbabwe played in three bilateral series within the next two seasons. Six Tests in 16 months. Between 2000 and 2005, India played 11 Tests against Zimbabwe and Bangladesh combined, of which they won nine and lost one.

AS: Yes, the luck of scheduling does play a part. In some ways Tendulkar's captaincy stint reminds me of Vengsarkar's in the 1980s. Ten Tests, five losses, two wins. However, seven of those Tests were against West Indies. India won the home series against New Zealand, but after the away series against West Indies, he was sidelined as unsuccessful. To be on the right side of the scheduling is important.

The series ends 2-0. In the final Test match, India have the upper hand. Dravid scores 148 and 81, they set a target of 356 and have the South Africans struggling at 95/7. But Cullinan and Klusener play out 117 minutes, giving full expression to their strokes and scoring 127. Srinath, Prasad and Kumble struggle to get the final breakthroughs and Cullinan hooks with nonchalance to finish unbeaten on 122.

Ganesh considers Cullinan the most difficult batsman he has bowled to.

With Donald in, the light deteriorates. The Indian management's pre-tour decision not to experiment with artificial lights comes back to bite them. The end score is 228/8. The match ends in a draw.

AM: India have played five Tests at the Wanderers at the time of writing and have never been beaten. Their record (two wins, three draws) is the best in any overseas ground where they have played four or more Tests anywhere outside Asia.

India have played six Tests in Georgetown and four in Antigua, all of which have been drawn. But the success ratio puts Wanderers at the top.

AS: Dravid scored his first Test century in the Wanderers Test. The first of an eventual 36. He stood there ignoring bouncer after bouncer, tiring the bowlers out.

AM: It took Dravid less than a year to secure that No. 3 slot from Ganguly. He would relinquish it to Laxman temporarily, and would open from time to time, but over the next 15 years he would largely bat first-down.

Unfortunately, he would manage only one more fifty in his three subsequent tours of South Africa. His average in South Africa would dip to under 30. However, in 2006/07 he would become the first Indian captain to win a Test match there.

With Dravid, Tendulkar and Azhar occupying three slots, only one of Laxman and Ganguly could be accommodated in the middle order. Ganguly scored two fifties at the Wanderers, while Laxman's thumb was fractured by a blow from Klusener.

That settled the odds in Ganguly's favour for the time being.

Laxman was forced to open the batting – a role he never enjoyed. Around the turn of the millennium, he made it clear that he would rather be dropped than open the batting in Test cricket. Thankfully, Azhar played his last Test match roughly around that time, which allowed Laxman to bat at five or six – something he would do till the end of his career.

His second-innings fifties and partnerships with Zaheer Khan would be crucial in India's first two wins on South African soil.

AS: In retrospect, Dravid's poor record in South Africa is not that surprising. His method of playing out the good balls and waiting for the bad ones did not work there apart from that one occasion. There were always too many good bowlers in South Africa and the conditions were always a bit too difficult. When you allowed the bowlers to bowl the way they wanted to, there was always bound to be a ball with your name on it. It is not surprising, as we mentioned earlier, when Tendulkar, and to a great extent Laxman, remained the consistent batsmen in South Africa.

Visiting batsmen in South Africa during 1996–2012

Batsman	M	R	Ave	SR	100	50
Adam Gilchrist	6	523	65.37	97.39	2	1
Chris Gayle	5	545	54.50	84.62	2	2
Phil Hughes	5	532	53.20	61.07	2	2
Andrew Strauss	9	826	51.62	50.86	3	2
Sachin Tendulkar	11	959	50.47	52.60	4	2
Stephen Fleming	8	697	49.78	57.46	1	3
Ricky Ponting	11	937	46.85	61.80	3	5
Brian Lara	9	841	46.72	54.75	2	5
Steve Waugh	6	408	45.33	40.15	1	2
Marcus Trescothick	5	448	44.80	52.33	2	0
Shivnarine Chanderpaul	11	799	42.05	40.41	2	5
VVS Laxman	10	566	40.42	47.48	0	4
Matthew Hayden	9	604	37.75	53.02	2	3
Sourav Ganguly	8	506	36.14	56.98	0	4
Kumar Sangakkara	8	572	35.75	48.68	1	3
Ridley Jacobs	9	462	33.00	45.29	0	3
Mike Hussey	8	449	32.07	42.35	0	4
Michael Vaughan	9	450	30.00	38.33	0	3
Rahul Dravid	11	624	29.71	37.63	1	2
Mahela Jayawardene	8	446	27.87	46.21	0	1

AS: From a cursory glance at the table we can see the low strike rates failing and high strike rates dominating. But, if we are a bit more scientific, we can compute the correlation coefficient between average and strike rate.

AM: The correlation coefficient tells us that for two sets of numbers, whether one increasing means the other increases, or decreases, or one's increase has no effect on the other. It takes a value between -1 and +1. If the value tends towards +1 it means when one variable rises, the other also rises. When it tends towards -1 it means one variable rising means the other decreases. When it is near 0, it means the rise or fall of the variables are independent of each other.

AS: When we compute the correlation coefficient between Average and Strike Rate of these visiting batsmen in South Africa, we find a value of +0.77, which is quite close to +1.

It means scoring quickly is strongly correlated with having a higher average. In short, quick scoring is generally more successful.

We must note that this same exercise for visiting batsmen in England produces a value very close to 0, which tells us there is no dependence between average and strike rate in England.

This also scientifically explains why Dravid was so successful in England while playing the same sort of game, but failed rather miserably in South Africa.

AM: The numbers for Dravid (average 29.71, strike rate 38) and Pujara (31.61 and 39) in South Africa are quite identical. They have a hundred (Dravid 148, Pujara 153) and two fifties each, and have failed more than they have succeeded.

The quicker scorers – Kohli, Tendulkar, Rahane (in his three Tests), Laxman, Kapil Dev, Ganguly – have all done better here.

On the other hand, while they have played one memorable innings each, Sehwag and Azhar have failed here – evidence that all-out attack might get runs here once in a while but not on a consistent basis.

Sustained aggression is perhaps the way to go here.

AS: Things remain pretty much the same in South Africa in the current day. The conditions have, if anything, turned more difficult. The 2017/18 tour saw some of the most challenging conditions for batting.

Contemporary Indian batsmen in South Africa

Batsman	M	R	Ave	SR	100	50
Virat Kohli	5	558	55.80	57.94	2	2
Ajinkya Rahane	3	266	53.20	49.52	0	2
Cheteshwar Pujara	7	411	31.61	38.88	1	2
Murali Vijay	6	278	23.16	34.62	0	1

AS: Coming back to the knocks by Azhar and Tendulkar in this innings. Both would count among the best innings played by visiting batsmen in South Africa. Speaking of best innings, this is a good time to list some of the greatest ever played there.

Greatest knocks in South Africa before the Indian tour 1996/97

AM: Plum Warner 132* Johannesburg 1898/99

After six colossal defeats in their first six Tests, this was the first time South Africa found themselves in a winning position. They bowled out England for 145 and secured a 106-run lead, and ten England batsmen managed 94 between them in the second innings. But they could not get past Warner, who, on debut, carried his bat with 132 not out. South Africa then collapsed for 99. That night, Lord Hawke presented Warner with a signet ring with the simple inscription: 'Lord Hawke's XI vs South Africa 1899. P.F.W., 132, from H'.

AS: Warwick Armstrong 159* Johannesburg 1902/03

For their first tour of South Africa, Australia arrived from a grand victorious 1902 summer of England. Suddenly they found themselves struggling to a draw in the first Test match, and in the second Test match they were behind by 65 in the first innings. In the second innings, Armstrong, a couple of decades before assuming the huge Big Ship dimensions, was dropped at point by Louis Tancred when on 25. After that the crisp shots were essayed with the impact of hammer strikes. A dust storm delayed play for half an hour and quick wickets were lost on resumption, but Armstrong was 94 not out by the end of the day and stretched it to 159 not out the next morning when the innings ended. Australia won by 159 runs. Armstrong was presented with the ball and a cigarette case by Buck Llewellyn.

AM: Jack (C.A.G.) Russell 140 and 111 Durban 1922/23

The first 'Jack' Russell to play for England, Charles Albert George scored two hundreds to help England seal the series 2-1. Phil Mead (66 in the first innings) was his only team-mate to get a fifty, and across the two innings, there were only two other scores in excess of 15. This was only the second time in history that a batsman scored two hundreds in the same Test match. Russell did not play again for England.

AS: Stan McCabe 189* Johannesburg 1935/36

McCabe took Australia to the brink of a remarkable win before a thunderstorm brought the game to an end. It was a superlative display of grace and power that almost achieved the magical. Chasing a near-impossible victory target of 399, Australia were 274/2 when South African captain Herby Wade appealed for the light. Yes, the fielding captain appealed for the light, and it was upheld because the umpires thought that the fieldsmen were in real physical danger from the balls that emerged from the middle of McCabe's willow and flashed past them under the cloudy skies. The players went off and a thundershower effectively ended the match.

AM: Neil Harvey 151* Durban 1949/50

Only once has a team won a Test match after not being asked to follow on despite conceding a lead of 200 runs. Bowled out for 99, Australia needed to chase 336 to win – and were reduced to 95/4, but Harvey, with Loxton and McCool for company, helped them to a five-wicket win. Harvey finished the tour with 660 runs and four hundreds – records for touring batsmen in a Test series in South Africa.

AS: Bert Sutcliffe 80* Johannesburg 1952/53

Neil Adcock generated frightening pace off the wicket. Sutcliffe wafted at one that thudded into the side of his head. He lost consciousness on the ground and at the hospital. His left ear split, he had a ghastly gash.

Lawrie Miller joined him there, coughing up blood after being hit on the chest. Both Sutcliffe and Miller were advised not to play any further.

Both did. His head swathed in bandage, Sutcliffe emerged at 81/4 and hooked the second ball he faced for six. He remained not out with 80, including seven sixes. The last-wicket partnership of 33 in 10 minutes with a heartbroken Bob Blair was the stuff of epics. That morning the team had received the news that Blair's fiancée had been killed in a train accident.

AM: John R. Reid 142 Johannesburg 1961/62

Under Reid, New Zealand came back from 0-1, then 1-2, to draw the series 2-2. Leading from the front, Reid became the first captain to score 500 runs and take ten wickets in a Test series. His finest performance came in the fourth Test. Trailing by 300, New Zealand were 38/3 when he came out. When he fell for a swashbuckling 142, the team score had advanced by only 184. It was during this innings that Jackie McGlew asked Tiger Lance to pray for Reid to get out, only for Lance to respond that it was probably God himself at the crease.

AS: Paul Barton 109 Port Elizabeth 1961/62

Barton had dislocated his shoulder trying to go for a catch in the Johannesburg Test match. At practice he tried to convince everyone that he was all right. But he had not been able to drive full tosses beyond silly mid-off. Captain John Reid's inclusion of him in the side was a giant gamble. He played a gem – 109 with 20 boundaries, most of them beautiful drives. Coming in at 20/2, he departed at 180/6. It was the high point of a career with a Test average of 20 and first-class numbers just a little better.

AM: Kapil Dev 129 Port Elizabeth 1992/93

This was the only Test match India lost in the series. Trailing by 63, they were undone by Donald (12-179), backed by Schultz, McMillan and Matthews. None of the first six Indian batsmen went past 7, but that did not matter to Kapil, who slammed 129. The second-highest score for the side, shared by three batsmen, was a mere 17. This was Kapil's last Test century.

AS: Michael Atherton 185* Johannesburg 1995/96

Writing about the innings in his autobiography, Atherton titled the chapter 'Johannesburg'. That was more than enough. Everyone knew what he meant. He also wrote the following sentence: 'If he is lucky, a batsman may once play an innings that defines him; one that, whether he likes it or not, he will be remembered for.'

This was the innings for Atherton: 643 minutes, 492 balls, many of them delivered by a seething, searing Donald. The only blemish was a chance on 99. He added an unbeaten 119 with Jack Russell in four hours and 34 minutes. Russell scored 29 not out. The match was miraculously saved – after Atherton's decision to put South Africa in on an apparently juicy surface had backfired. Kirsten, new to the Test side, supposedly thought, 'Hold on, maybe I could also do this one day.'

AM: And Kirsten did. Since the Tendulkar–Azhar show, then there have been some extraordinary knocks. It makes sense to list them as well.

AT THE END OF THE DAY

Mark Waugh 116 Port Elizabeth 1996/97

Junior Waugh's finest Test innings.

From 30/2 in pursuit of 270.

Australia won by two wickets and eventually levelled the series.

Azhar Mahmood 132/Saeed Anwar 118 Durban 1997/98

Mahmood was in at 89/5 and last out at 259, scoring 132 out of 170.

His last four partners got 14 runs between them while adding 132.

All that against Donald, Pollock, de Villiers and Klusener.

In the second innings Anwar got 118 with only Aamer Sohail managing any semblance of resistance at the other end.

Brian Lara 202 Johannesburg 2002/03

Coming in at 94/2, Lara lifted West Indies to 410.

None of his team-mates went past 60.

A world record 28 runs came in an over from Robin Peterson.

Andrew Strauss 126 and 94* Port Elizabeth 2004/05

Strauss utilised contrasting approaches in the two innings.

Patience was the key in the first but with rain threatening, he went for strokes to chase down the target in the second.

Sachin Tendulkar 146 Cape Town 2010/11

The duel of the decade. Tendulkar vs Steyn.

Tendulkar got a hundred and Steyn got five wickets.

Steyn was at his best. Tendulkar had to be, to get that century.

Michael Clarke 151 Cape Town 2011/12

A miraculous effort with Steyn, Morkel and Philander on fire.

Clarke got his hundred in 108 balls while the top six managed a combined strike rate of less than 30. No one else crossed 44.

David Warner 135 and 145/Michael Clarke 161* Cape Town 2013/14

Clarke was hit on the ribs, then on his elbow with an audible crunch. The next ball broke a nail on his thumb. Five balls later he was cracked on the jaw.

He was tested for concussion. The next day he borrowed an arm guard from Chris Rogers and walked out to score one of the bravest hundreds in the history of Test cricket.

So intense was Clarke's hundred that Warner's twin tons went almost unnoticed.

Ben Stokes 258 Cape Town 2015/16

It was brutal – 258 off 198 balls with 30 boundaries and 11 sixes.

In the midst of the exhilarating belligerence, childhood friend Jonny Bairstow scored his own maiden Test match hundred.

'The ball is travelling so far, that South Africa might be better off posting a couple of fielders on Table Mountain,' was Bairstow's version in his autobiography co-authored by Duncan Hamilton.

Virat Kohli 153 Centurion 2017/18

Kohli's series tally was 286 runs. None of his team-mates reached 120.

A combination of concentration and survival skills were combined with breathtaking strokes against the four-pronged pace attack.

He restrained his strokes as he lost partners, yet scored at a strike rate in excess of 70.

Kusal Perera 153* Durban 2018/19

Sri Lanka found themselves 226/9 facing a target of 304.

Kusal Perera, then on 86, expertly farmed the strike while bringing off outrageous sixes and reverse-swept boundaries.

His fifth six, off Steyn no less, brought the target down to single figures, and a steer off Rabada ended the most remarkable chase in Test cricket.

AS: The best innings by overseas batsmen in South Africa are all special. The land remains one of the most difficult places to bat. And the bowlers have continued to get better.

Another innings from the post-isolation era that comes to my mind was during the first Test match India played in South Africa. Pravin Amre scored a superb century on debut at Durban.

AM: Yes, that one definitely merits special mention. Amre made his ODI debut in South Africa's first international match after their readmission to international cricket, and scored a crucial fifty. Then, with this hundred at Durban, he became the second cricketer in history to score a fifty on ODI debut and a hundred on Test debut.

Interestingly, Kepler Wessels, the first to achieve this 'double', played for South Africa in Amre's international debut matches, even leading them in the Test match. Of course, Wessels's Test and ODI debuts had come for Australia.

AS: Amre's century on his Test debut led match referee Clive Lloyd to say that he was another in the long line of great Indian batsmen. However, surprisingly, he had a very short career. He did not really fail ... he was never even given a chance to do so. One of the players done in by curious, inexplicable selection policies. In fact, he had an end to his Test career even less explainable than Vinod Kambli, the third Indian batsman from coach Ramakant Achrekar's stable alongside Tendulkar and Amre.

AM: Amre's entire Test career spanned less than nine months. As you said, he was never given a chance to fail. His last seven innings in Test cricket read 12, 78, 57, 52*, 21, 15*, 21. He ended with an average of 42.50, without really doing much to lose his place in the side.

As for Kambli, he had just one ordinary series, against Walsh and co. in 1994/95, before he was discarded.

AS: Somehow the perception is that Kambli failed in a number of Tests, his weakness was exposed, and he was a poor overseas traveller. The fact is that he did have a problem with the short ball, but not something that cannot be rectified or lived with through a career, as some others were allowed to do later on. He played just one Test match outside Asia, in New Zealand in 1993/94. And what irks most is that he hardly got a chance to bat in his last series, because it was thoroughly disrupted by rain. For someone who ended with an average of nearly 60 in first-class cricket, he was not given even a fraction of the rope handed out to many a big name in Indian cricket.

AM: One cannot help but wonder whether Kambli was dropped too soon. He was certainly good enough to play for Boland in the Currie Cup, in 2002/03. Of his team-mates, only Con de Lange (who later played international cricket for Scotland) scored more runs that season. Boland had also signed up Amre, in 1999/2000. Unfortunately, Amre did not impress during his stint.

AS: That is a unique Indian connection to South Africa, Amre and Kambli playing in the Currie Cup. Indian cricketers have played on the county circuit for a long, long time. Rusi Surti played in the Sheffield Shield. However, the Currie Cup had, for very obvious reasons, remained outside the realms of Indians. These two bridged that gap.

AM: In fact, very few Indians have played domestic first-class cricket outside India and the British Isles.

Subhash Gupte and Robin Singh played in the West Indies, but that never overlapped with their careers for India.

Apart from Surti, Emmanuel Benjamin played for Tasmania, but he was not an international cricketer. Neither was Digvijay Amarnath (son of Surinder), whose entire first-class career was for two Sri Lankan teams.

And Rahul Dravid, VVS Laxman, Amit Mishra, Lakshmipathy Balaji, and Dhawal Kulkarni playing in New Zealand in 2009 was a one-off attempt at providing the Test match specialists with practice before a Test series.

AS: Given the limited cricketing interaction between India and South Africa, the teams have played each other pretty regularly since the re-admission of the latter – 15 series and 39 Tests over 28 years until 2020. Only England and Australia have played more against South Africa and that can be related, factually and symbolically, as a combined reflection of the imperial past and commercial present.

The next time India visited South Africa, they floundered as usual at 68/4 on the first morning before Tendulkar and Sehwag put together that blistering partnership. They struggled in the second Test match as well. And then of course, there was the other great event of the tour. The infamous Mike Denness affair.

The Mike Denness affair

Port Elizabeth Test, 2001.

Shiv Sunder Das and Virender Sehwag were fielding close in and seemed to go up, in the opinion of the umpires, for everything. So did wicketkeeper Deep Dasgupta. All three young, enthusiastic newcomers to the side. Four players were fined 75% of their match fees – Dasgupta, Das, Sehwag and the off-spinner Harbhajan Singh.

When the umpires reported them, Dasgupta, Das and Harbhajan were handed suspended one-Test bans.

Besides, Sehwag had latched on to a ball that the umpires thought bounced off the ground. The fielders thought it had come off the boot of Jacques Kallis after he had played it defensively. Sehwag had charged towards the umpire, appealing loudly and had uttered a frustrated curse when the decision had been not out. 'Crude and abusive language,' had been the official version. What he had used was the oft-repeated f-word.

Denness banned Sehwag for the final Test match.

He also fined Sourav Ganguly 75% of his match fee because of his lack of control over the team.

AS: The first of the allegations was excessive appealing. A series of ear-splitting appeals were indulged in, started mostly by the excitable Harbhajan Singh and picked up by the chorus of close-in fielders. Mike Denness was also miffed that captain Sourav Ganguly did not wave his captain's baton and rein in his men.

AM: Not that excessive appealing was a new allegation. That had been a constant complaint against the Indian side by many an official. However, the South Africans had been no saints themselves and had gone scot-free. Or rather there had been no undue fuss made of this very normal part of the game. The difference in treatment was quite palpable.

AS: Besides, the decision to ban Sehwag seemed rather atrocious to most. Especially with the images of Ricky Ponting and the other Australians going full blast with their colourful vocabularies being fresh in the memory, nothing really left to the imagination with cameras close enough for successful lip-reading and receptive stump microphones. That was going overboard and sympathy was quite understandably in favour of the two-Test-old batsman.

AM: But the last straw was the allegation against Tendulkar. Not reported by the umpires, but purely a Denness initiative. One with a hitherto unblemished record in his 12-year career, the demigod to millions was accused of tampering with the ball, docked 75% of his match fee and handed a suspended one-match ban.

On the third day, with Srinath and Agarkar dismissing three batsmen for just 26, Ganguly and

213

Tendulkar had come on as the third and fourth seamers. Tendulkar had immediately started moving the ball more than anyone.

AS: By itself that was not indicative of anything suspicious. After all, when he bowled leg spin he turned it more than any spinner in India. However, when on the instruction of the local TV producer the cameramen zoomed in on Tendulkar's grip, he was spotted doing something to the seam. The replays and analysis went on an overdrive.

Denness asked for the tapes. The explanation was that Tendulkar was cleaning the ball. He booked the master batsman for not informing the umpires that he was cleaning the ball, under Law 42.3 (b). The charge was not tampering.

When Denness informed the Indian team of suspended one-match bans for Tendulkar, Ganguly, Das, Dasgupta and Harbhajan, and a one-match ban for Sehwag which prevented him from playing the third Test match, the infuriated cricketers leaked the news to the media.

AM: As a public outcry resulted, including accusations of bias and even racism against Denness, the Indians took the field on the final day to play out time in the rain-affected Test match. On air, several commentators, primarily Navjot Sidhu, blasted Denness openly.

AS: Meanwhile, Denness did himself no favours by refusing to answer questions while facing journalists in the end-of-match press conference. Ravi Shastri, working as a commentator and not really one to attend press conferences as a journalist, was nevertheless present for this one. Infuriated by a silent Denness, he asked, 'If Mike Denness cannot answer questions, why is he here? We all know what he looks like.'

It was a mistake for Denness to be there in the press conference. He had been asked by Gerald Majola, CEO of UCBSA, to accompany him in order to defuse the potentially explosive situation. However, ICC regulations prevented him from discussing the matter. So, his silent presence did anything but defuse the situation.

While the ICC backed Denness, the Indian board president Jagmohan Dalmiya stood staunchly behind his players. He demanded Denness be sacked. Niranjan Shah, honorary secretary of the BCCI, commented: 'We are unhappy with his inconsistency and the India team have no confidence in him. We feel that all the decisions are against only India. The South Africans committed the same excessive appealing.'

The ICC refused.

AS: And suddenly it was the 1960s yet again, with the cricket boards around the world divided along colour lines. The English, Australian and New Zealand boards supported the ICC and Denness, while the others backed the BCCI.

Malcolm Speed [then ICC president] was rather standoffish while rebuffing the Indian journalists. He faced them while changing planes in Mumbai. 'Rules are there for a reason,' he said, with an audible shrug of sorts. Somewhat harking back to the days of getting rid of the usual beggars and urchins when a white man stopped over in the subcontinental shores during long journeys.

AM: Ehsan Mani (Pakistan-born businessman and then ICC president-elect), commented that while there was no racism involved: 'What we have is an enormous communication problem. There is also a big cultural gap between Asian culture and white culture.' This was perhaps closer to the truth than Speed's statement.

AS: Indeed, South Africa was the last place where a controversy divided on colour lines should have erupted. I remember the media in India were going ballistic.

An editorial in the generally balanced Hindu thundered: 'Denness's sense of fairness dates back to the Victorian era when Britannia ruled the waves. In the event, Denness truly believes – in the manner of his forefathers who ruled this land with such cunning for so long – that there are always two sets of rules. Nothing has changed since the days when the sun never set on the British Empire.' The Indian politicians got a whiff of a juicy piece of news and everyone was soon snapping for a bite.

AM: And while the crisis threatened to rip the cricket world in two, Dalmiya was accused of using the issue to get back at his old ICC adversaries.

AS: Scyld Berry described Dalmiya as 'the control freak, the player of political games, the man who destabilises then poses as the saviour of the Indian tour by telling his players to play on'. On the other hand, Harsha Bhogle, who himself had been rather self-confessedly emotional while on air the morning of the fifth day, said that Dalmiya was 'a reflection of the Indian mood'.

The impasse was not one that looked likely to be resolved. The scrapping of the third Test match would result in huge financial loss for the South African board and put future cricketing relations between the two countries in jeopardy.

BCCI and UCBSA presented a united front, asking for the sacking of Denness. However, the ICC would not relent.

With reports of protests in front of the South African embassy in New Delhi coming in, the government got involved.

The two boards, backed by their two governments, sent Denness packing and replaced him with former South African wicketkeeper Denis Lindsay.

Speed was vitriolic: 'No cricket board has the authority to remove Denness from his position as match referee. The ICC cannot accede to demands for his removal. To remove him under this kind of pressure would be to disregard the rules agreed by all member countries and set an unacceptable precedent. It has been suggested in South Africa that a replacement match could be staged if the Test does not go ahead. If this were to happen it would not be recognised by the ICC as a Test match. It would not be officiated by an ICC referee or umpire and neither the result nor statistics would be included in Test match records.'

AS: In Kolkata, where burning effigies is a passionate pastime, such honours were bestowed on Denness.

The former England captain remained upbeat. 'I am in the good company of George Bush and Tony Blair.' When local hero Sourav Ganguly was dropped in 2006 after several poor seasons, the then Indian coach Greg Chappell joined this select group.

Indeed, Denness put on a brave face, taciturnly remarking: 'I certainly won't be going to the ground on Friday.'

AM: It is not that Denness took a stand. Had he indeed gone to the ground, authorities would have stopped him from entering. And he had been made aware of that.

The match itself was a damp squib, with South Africa easily winning the unofficial 'Test'.

AM: An all-South African team playing a touring team in an unofficial 'Test'. Not the sort of déjà vu they would have wanted.

AS: Ganguly suddenly developed a crick in the neck and sat out. Connor Williams batted pretty well in that 'Test'. He never played for India in an official Test match.

However, my abiding memory of that match is Shaun Pollock bouncing and Harbhajan playing him defensively with the straightest of bats, the bottom of the blade pointing heavenwards and the handle towards the ground.

AM: That was not the end of it. With Sehwag's ban still standing, the issue was brought to the fore once again with England visiting India.

AS: There was some posturing by Dalmiya. When things remained a bit fuzzy, Speed asked him whether Sehwag would play in the Mohali Test. Dalmiya's response was that the request for such information violated the playing conditions, adding further that it might have to be investigated by the ICC's Anti-Corruption Unit. A real Dalmiya moment.

Denness served as match referee in two more Tests and three ODIs. He was not re-appointed by the ICC the following year. He insisted that it was because, 'There was a reduction from the part-time referees, of which I was one, to the full-time referees.'

AS: Sitting as we do now 19 years after the incident, would you say there was a bias involved in the decisions rolled out by Denness? And if there was, did it seem racially motivated?

AM: It is difficult to say. What Sehwag did at Port Elizabeth was certainly not anything as obnoxious as the body language we saw from Michael Slater when Rahul Dravid did not leave the crease at Mumbai in 2000/01. And yet, Sehwag was banned for a match by Denness. Slater got away.

AS: In my opinion – and I have no way of verifying it but will embellish it through anecdotal evidence – there might not have been something overtly racial, but rather a case of unfamiliarity.

During the telecast, I remember the commentators repeatedly showing the appeals of Shaun Pollock, which seemed as vociferous but went unpunished.

There was no real difference between the way he appealed and the way the Indians appealed, but there is the case of one being familiar to one eye and the other being not. Every culture has its way of expressing themselves. What may look aggressive to one culture, or objectionable, may be perfectly normal to another. And if we switch the observer and actor, the same is true for the other side.

So, for Denness, and the umpires Russell Tiffin and Ian Howell, a young, warm-blooded white athlete like Pollock appealing in that manner was perhaps something completely normal. That is how boys will be and that sort of thing. But the facial expressions of Sehwag and the other Indians, as they appealed, could have seemed unfamiliar and oddly threatening or lewd in a subliminal way.

It is a natural reaction, and very uncomfortable to talk about in these politically correct days. However, this is a major cause of cultural misunderstanding.

In a way this is indeed a stepping stone to most racial problems.

AM: If you ask me, it is difficult for anyone to find S.S. Das – arguably the most innocent-looking cricketer to have played for India – even remotely threatening, but each to one's own, I suppose.

AS: Thankfully, the UCBSA and BCCI ensured that cricketing relations were maintained between the two nations. Of course, everyone was aware of the financial potential of the Indian market when it comes to cricket. And the World Cup was just a year away and scheduled in South Africa. A dream World Cup from the sponsors' point of view, with India making the final with Tendulkar being the star of the show most of the way.

AM: Unlike Pollock in the Super Sixes match against Sri Lanka in the World Cup, UCBSA got their calculations right.

As for the World Cup, it was a resounding success despite their early exit. Co-hosts Kenya saw to that.

AS: And then a few years later South Africa hosted the inaugural Twenty20 World Cup.

AM: India, sans Tendulkar, Ganguly and Dravid, and without a coach, went on to lift the inaugural edition of the trophy. Few had expected them to win, though the percentage was certainly higher than the ones who backed them to win the 1983 World Cup.

In less than six months' time, the auctions of the inaugural editions of the IPL were held. The money associated with the tournament was unprecedented in the history of cricket.

AS: In 2009 the IPL coincided with the Assembly Elections of India. With security being a problem with the unwanted mix of these two major Indian mega events, the IPL was shifted to South Africa.

In retrospect, the BCCI–UCBSA alliance was a very, very fruitful one.

AS: The Mike Denness affair was not an easy situation to deal with. Especially in South Africa.

AM: Well, not too many things have been easy in the aftermath of apartheid – as we discussed, over-compensation, the quota system, over-sensitivity. These are unavoidable appendages and unfortunately have done some internal harm to South African cricket.

AS: Yes, we have spoken of the quota system. With Kolpak there was a way out.

Kolpak

Back in 2000, Maroš Kolpak, a Slovak handball player and a German citizen, was released by the German team TSV Östringen on the grounds that they had already completed their quota of two non-EU citizens.

Kolpak challenged the German Handball Association on grounds of discrimination against him. The case went through the German higher court to the European Court of Justice. He won the case in 2003.

Since then, citizens of countries with 'applicable Association Agreements with the EU' who are working in an EU country have had equal rights to work as EU citizens. This included European countries as well as South Africa, Zimbabwe, some Caribbean nations, Papua New Guinea, and others.

The practice was soon adapted by athletes in other sports, especially cricket and rugby. With its many first-class teams and a competitive pay scale, English counties provided lucrative career opportunities for overseas cricketers, especially white South Africans, some of whom found it hard to break through the quota system of their country.

The England and Wales Cricket Board (ECB) tried to counter this by imposing penalties on the counties (£85 in one-day matches and £340 in County Championship matches) per Kolpak player. In 2007 they raised it to £275 and £1,100 respectively. It did not work.

In a match between Northamptonshire and Leicestershire in 2008, 13 of the 22 players were overseas-born; of them, 11 were Kolpak cricketers. The sixth Leicestershire wicket, Claude Henderson c Andrew Hall b Johan van der Wath, involved three men who had already played for South Africa (in 2004, Henderson had become the first cricketer to sign up under Kolpak rulings).

While Zimbabwe and the West Indies faced some blows, South Africa got the worst of it. Faf du Plessis, Ryan McLaren and Jacques Rudolph did return after renouncing their respective Kolpak offers, but most others did not follow suit.

Andrew Hall, Colin Ingram, Alviro Petersen, Hardus Viljoen, Simon Harmer, Ashwell Prince, Stiaan van Zyl, David Wiese, Marchant de Lange, Heino Kuhn, Wayne Parnell, Duanne Olivier, Morne Morkel – the list is long.

The most significant among these names is Kyle Abbott. Having to battle Steyn, Philander, Morkel and Rabada for a fast bowler's spot is not easy. Abbott played 11 Tests over a period of four years, picking up 39 wickets at 22.71. Having to warm the reserve bench got to him after a while.

Abbott was replaced by Vernon Philander for the 2015 World Cup semi-final against New Zealand. It was a surprise decision, because Abbott had taken nine wickets from four matches in the tournament till then, at 14.44, while conceding just 4.19 an over.

Philander did not do well as his side went down fighting against New Zealand. Sections of the South African media suggested that Philander was chosen over Abbott to adhere to the quota system, against the wishes of captain A.B. de Villiers.

In his autobiography, de Villiers explained that while the decision could have been taken entirely for cricketing reasons, it seemed to him that 'there could have been other considerations'. Cricket South Africa (CSA) denied the claim that it was a throwback to Justin Ontong's selection over Jacques Rudolph in 2001/02.

Abbott later confessed that he had been very close to retirement from international cricket at that point. He finally took the decision in 2017. Becoming the spearhead of the Hampshire attack, he entered the record books in 2019 when he picked up 17-86 against Somerset – the best match figures since Jim Laker's 19-90.

Harsh? Perhaps. White South African cricketers are bearing the brunt. Cricket South Africa will lose more cricketers (unless Brexit changes the equation). However, if one looks at the bigger picture, the quota system is perhaps likely to cause more good than harm to South African cricket – and society – in the long run.

It will not be a bad idea to see how white South African cricketers of the 1970s and 1980s coped with the isolation that dried up opportunities in their days and the events that transpired thereafter.

Peter Pollock, as is evident from the title of his autobiography *God's Fast Bowler*, took to religion. His younger brother Graeme acknowledged the evils of the era, admitting that they should have done more for people who were deprived of opportunities they deserved. Ali Bacher and Mike Procter were among those who took the lead in helping eradicate racism from South African sport even before their re-admission.

While some are still struggling to come to terms with being deprived, better sense has generally prevailed, and as a result, the world is a far better place to live in. The white cricketers of the current generation have some excellent role models to look up to.

AS: The dynamics have been complex. It was not as if the end of apartheid meant the end of racism in the truest sense. If we do not close our eyes and ears to the revelations of Makhaya Ntini and others during the Black Lives Matter movement of 2020, we do realise that the culture of segregation ran deep enough to create implicit and also sometimes crude barriers in the side.

AM: Had Lungi Ngidi not announced that he would take the knee to support the Black Lives Matter stance, one wonders how many of these stories would have surfaced. From Makhaya Ntini to Ashwell Prince to Robin Peterson to Aya Mayoli, coloured cricketers have come out with their experiences of being at the receiving end of discrimination. Paul Adams has been quite vocal in the movement as well.

AS: Looking back, it was quite expected. I don't mean to say it was desired in any way, but it was expected that the years and years of segregation would have an effect. It is cultural inertia. The differences due to colour, colonial past, erstwhile empire on which the sun never set ... all these have been facts of the past. And there have been plenty of measures taken to eradicate the same around the world. But it has taken time. At the systemic and subliminal level, it still exists and cannot be denied. From the stewards of Lord's to the ivory towers of the 'prestigious' cricket magazines, everyone tries to adapt himself to a colour-blind modern world, but they still stumble big time due to unawareness of the changing parameters. The experience of Ntini and the others is just a manifestation of the same.

Paul Adams on the Black Lives Matter movement

When you are playing, enjoying yourself, it does seem okay … but then you reflect and wonder why progress has not really taken place.

Our society has not really been taken to a level where sport is encouraged. Sport has disappeared from the schools in the townships. Sporting bodies don't have the resources to perform the transformation through sports that had originally been expected.

We have had glimpses of what sport can do to a society, when the rugby team won the World Cup. But we require real successful transformation with help from the government and the corporate sectors if we want to achieve change through sport.

AM: The response of most South African white cricketers of the 1990s or the 2000s to the Black Lives Matter movement has been refreshing. Unfortunately, there have been exceptions to this, a clear indication that the stigma had not been eradicated entirely with the end of the apartheid era.

While that is unfortunate, things are definitely looking up as the generation born and brought up after 1994 are taking charge in various spheres of life.

AS: While the generation born and brought up after 1994 have not seen legalised apartheid first hand, they have indeed seen the aftermath ... which is a disturbed society, with throwbacks and a sense of injustice and unrest. And it also works the other way. If someone has not witnessed it first hand, and has not bothered to look up the history of that period, it is difficult to fathom the reasons behind the polarisation of opinions and the extremely strong reactions.

As Michael Holding very poignantly pointed out in the Sky TV production on Black Lives Matter, the awareness of what has gone on in history is very important for people to understand what was wrong and to address the same. Without that we will forever ask and answer the wrong questions.

AM: John Arlott was probably the biggest exception to this. It did not take Arlott long to figure out exactly what was wrong with South African society. Arlott had made his stance clear when he wrote 'Human' in the entry next to 'Race' on the South African immigration form. He wrote about the situation extensively. Some of his experiences seem almost unreal today.

Had Arlott not been vocal about his stance, one cannot help but wonder whether D'Oliveira would have reached out to him.

AS: Arlott was an exception in the 1940s and 1950s. It is strange that all these years later, in our supposed enlightened day and age, there are still writers and commentators who are not aware of what went on in South Africa's past, still forget to pen the details of the roots of the apartheid problem. They probably are still under the impression that the past segregation issues were teething problems of backward tribal people suddenly asking for equal rights. And therefore, even now when writing about the South African isolation from 1970 to 1991, they parrot the same question: 'Was it okay to mix politics with sport?' That is the problem of lack of awareness of history. The questions of basic human rights, oppression and subjugation are then bracketed under 'politics'. Examples of such apathy are plentiful.

AM: Some of the then contemporary names in the British cricket fraternity made it very clear, through inaction or otherwise, that they did not want to interfere in the affairs of South Africa. Denis Compton's name immediately jumps to mind. Married to a South African, Compton spent more time, and therefore knew more, of South African society than most of his contemporaries.

When Compton scored that 300 at Benoni in 1948/49, the black section of the crowd had gone ballistic, cheering every stroke. There was no possible way that he could not have noticed how they were segregated, almost caged, even as they watched the game. It simply did not seem to register as an important enough detail.

Even in the 1980s, post-Biko, during extreme racial problems, Compton was still trying to pull strings and arrange official tours to South Africa.

AS: It is about being used to a system, however unreasonable, so that in retrospect it looks incredible that it carried on. For example, it was 1998 before women were allowed in the premises of the pavilion at Lord's. People were so used to this ridiculous rule that they had not questioned a stance that would be crucified in any sane society. The foreign cricketers like Compton who travelled to South Africa, and even the white cricketers who settled there ... they lived in a white bubble. Things were not only normal within the bubble, things were magnificent. They did not question it.

AM: Still on Compton. To be fair, he did visit black townships and trained the children there. However, as Tim Heald wrote in Compton's biography, 'his South African friends treated their [coloured] servants just as upper-class English people would treat their servants'.

Few things demonstrate more than this why the definition of ethics was fundamentally problematic during Compton's era. He, just like his contemporaries, never realised that they had little right to assume that the black population was there to serve their ilk.

AS: Is it common knowledge yet? Privilege and segregation are politically incorrect today. But they do take different forms. For example, except for Vasant Raiji on Trumper, and Mihir Bose on Keith Miller, it is very difficult to think of books on white cricket by non-white writers that have been acknowledged by the ivory towers of cricket writing. Non-white writers are generally acknowledged if they stick to non-white cricket (if they do not go beyond a boundary).

AM: It does not work the other way, though. Some of the most wonderful books written on cricket in the subcontinent have been by white writers. They have found universal acclaim. Richard Cashman's seminal *Patrons, Players, and the Crowd*, Scyld Berry's *Cricket Wallah*, Peter Oborne's two classics on Pakistan cricket, Tim Albone's *Out of the Ashes* ...

AS: Although, in a globalised world, there is no reason to believe that the other direction cannot be traversed by the non-white writers. But for non-white cricket writers it has been quite a struggle to get recognised in that domain, historically marked out for white writers. Maybe a case of politically incorrect and uncomfortable truth. But rather undeniable.

AM: Ali Bacher played a key role in accommodating the black population into mainstream cricket. However, with time it became evident that the inclusion of the odd black cricketer would not be enough to address the problem. A quota system was the logical way to resolve this swiftly: it had already been left too late.

AS: The quota system perhaps had to be introduced to aid the levelling of the playing field. As Jonty Rhodes recently said, 'I certainly benefited from the fact that I wasn't really competing with 50% of the population.'

But the quota system did have its drawbacks. We have already talked about Kevin Pietersen and the other examples of talented white cricketers losing out. At the same time, as Ashwell Prince recently pointed out, even when the black cricketer performed better than or on a par with the white cricketer, the stigma of being coloured – and hence a supposed quota cricketer – still stuck to him.

AM: Then there have been the controversies. Eyebrows were raised after Justin Ontong was picked ahead of Jacques Rudolph and Vernon Philander over Kyle Abbott. While there is little doubt that the quota system was necessary, one cannot help but wonder whether some adjustments are in order.

AS: Of course, apart from the quota system there are other problems linked to South African society that become a major reason for the opposition to the Black Lives Matter movement that we see in some of the past cricketers. The violence that is almost daily fare, the insecurity, the rich-poor divide, the recent spate of farm murders. All these play their roles. It is a very troubled society and the complicated past has definitely not helped matters.

AM: As Holding pointed out, the correct way forward is to educate oneself on the history of racial – and other – injustice. Society needs to acknowledge its errors and go out of its way to rectify its ways. And that is precisely why Faf du Plessis' statement – 'all lives won't matter unless Black Lives Matter' – resonates so much.

AS: In that context, the frequent India–South Africa contests come across as extremely important, doing a great deal to undo the segregated history of the past. South Africa have played India 39 times since re-admission, won 15 and lost 14. It is a rivalry that started in 1992/93 and can be said to be one of the greatest modern contests. In recent times, two series played in India have been one-sided, but otherwise most of the rubbers have been keenly contested.

AM: The one-sided series in India, however, do not give them an upper hand. South Africa have won (a whitewash, no less) a series on Indian soil, but India are yet to repay that favour.

AS: One just hopes that the dynamics brought about by quota and Kolpak do not take the competitive edge out of the Protean outfits of the future.

The two teams have provided some magnificent action down the years. From the first ever third-umpire decision in Test cricket to Sreesanth breaking into his impromptu dance after hitting Andre Nel for six to the iconic Tendulkar–Steyn clash ... and many more.

AM: While Indians have a dedicated following across the world, South Africans, too, have been cheered by Indian fans – for an assortment of reasons.

A packed Eden Gardens welcomed the South Africans back to international cricket.

Fifteen years later, the same crowd cheered South Africa against India – because Ganguly, the local star, had been dropped.

Chants of 'Ey-Bee-Dee' reverberated across Wankhede Stadium as de Villiers romped to another incredible hundred.

AS: The India–South Africa rivalry is special, even more so because it started in relatively equal circumstances. If we consider Australia or England, they had been cricketing superpowers when India came into the fold, and the new cricketing nation had a lot of catching up to do.

AM: When India and South Africa clashed for the first time in Test cricket, South Africa was placed at the most crucial juncture in their history. The Indians, on the other hand, were a team emerging into a new era, reflecting the opening of the economy and globalisation.

AS: The 1990s saw the birth of a new India. There had been the awakening brought about by globalisation, which reflected in the commercial deals struck around cricket. Almost as a necessity, helped along by some incredibly talented cricketers, boundaries had been redefined, first by Tendulkar and down the decade by a gamut of new cricketers who believed they could compete at the global level and win regularly – rather than being the perennial underdogs with their precious once-in-a-blue-moon victories bubble-wrapped with numerous fables.

And South Africa was returning to the international fold. Not that their cricket had suffered due to the absence, as they re-emerged as one of the best sides. But, they were not quite sure that they would start off as one of the best. There was the natural apprehension of fitting in at the highest level. The result was that the two sides took on one another as virtual equals, which led to magnificent contests.

AM: This partnership came at a very crucial juncture. If one combines the two home-and-away series, the Tests were tied two-all when the teams came to Cape Town. While Azhar and Tendulkar could not prevent a defeat, they certainly helped instil a fighting spirit in India. The six-match contest ended with light conditions standing between India and a 3-3 outcome.

AS: Perhaps if India had succumbed in a Durbanesque 100 and 66 manner at Cape Town, the initiative would have been wrested by the South Africans once and for all in the rivalry. Early and decisive. At 58/5 in reply to 529/7 declared, there was every indication of an almighty surrender. As G. Viswanath later put it, the partnership showed that the Indians could compete.

Hence, as we discussed, it was an extraordinary partnership, a backs-to-the-wall counterattack from both ends never seen in Indian cricket before or since, in the presence of Nelson Mandela, in that colourful country, the incredible historical undertones and in an epochal moment of world cricket ... It had drama all around it. Volumes should have been written about it through the years. And somehow we have to dig deep to find even a report.

AM: As cricket, especially batting, becomes more and more aggressive, with greater focus on quick scoring, we may be privileged enough to witness similar stands where two great batsmen, with all odds stacked against them, will come at a rampant pace attack all guns blazing at both ends to pull off yet another partnership that will stand the test of time.

AS: There is no doubt Alletson deserved a book on his innings. It was an incredible knock, seldom seen before or since. So did Kippax and Hooker on their partnership. These deeds needed to be remembered, amidst all the sound and fury of televised and repeat-televised bombardment of modern cricket.

However, this association between two of the best batsmen of the game at the highest level required a volume on it as well. Since there was no Arlott writing the story, no Ross penning down the second *Cape Summer*, it was left to us.

Match scorecard

SECOND TEST: NEWLANDS, CAPE TOWN, 2–6 JANUARY 1997

TOSS: SOUTH AFRICA

South Africa	First innings		B	4	6
Andrew Hudson	c Mongia b Prasad	16	52	1	
Gary Kirsten	run out (Azharuddin/ Ganguly)	103	204	15	
Adam Bacher	c Mongia b Srinath	25	60	4	
Daryll Cullinan	c Mongia b Prasad	77	141	6	1
*Hansie Cronje	c Mongia b Srinath	41	79	3	1
Brian McMillan	not out	103	233	9	
Shaun Pollock	c Tendulkar b Prasad	1	13		
†Dave Richardson	c Dravid b Srinath	39	106	5	
Lance Klusener	not out	102	100	13	1
Allan Donald					
Paul Adams					
Extras	(5 b, 9 lb, 8 nb)	22			
Total	(7 wickets declared, 162.5 overs)	529			

Fall of wickets: 1-37 (Hudson), 2-89 (Bacher), 3-203 (Kirsten), 4-251 (Cullinan), 5-291 (Cronje), 6-299 (Pollock), 7-382 (Richardson)

India bowling: Srinath 38-8-130-3, Prasad 36-1-114-3, Ganesh 23.5-6-93-0, Kumble 51-7-136-0, Ganguly 9-1-24-0, Raman 5-1-18-0

SACHIN AND AZHAR AT CAPE TOWN

India	First innings		B	4	6
W.V. Raman	run out (Klusener)	5	11	1	
Rahul Dravid	b Klusener	2	41		
Sourav Ganguly	c McMillan b Donald	23	38	2	
Venkatesh Prasad	b Adams	0	2		
*Sachin Tendulkar	c Bacher b McMillan	169	254	26	
VVS Laxman	c Richardson b Pollock	5	23	1	
Mohammad Azharuddin	run out (Hudson)	115	110	19	1
†Nayan Mongia	lbw b Adams	5	31	1	
Anil Kumble	c Richardson b Donald	2	18		
Javagal Srinath	b Pollock	11	27	1	
Dodda Ganesh	not out	2	11		
Extras	(9 lb, 11 nb)	20			
Total	(all out, 92.2 overs)	359			

Fall of wickets: 1-7 (Raman), 2-24 (Dravid), 3-25 (Prasad), 4-33 (Ganguly), 5-58 (Laxman), 6-280 (Azharuddin), 7-298 (Mongia), 8-315 (Kumble), 9-340 (Srinath), 10-359 (Tendulkar)

South Africa bowling: Donald 24-3-99-2, Pollock 23-2-76-2, Adams 18-5-49-2, Klusener 12-1-88-1, McMillan 6.2-0-22-1, Cronje 9-5-16-0

South Africa	Second innings		B	4	6
Andrew Hudson	b Srinath	55	134	7	
Gary Kirsten	lbw b Ganesh	0	10		
Adam Bacher	lbw b Srinath	0	3		
Lance Klusener	c Dravid b Srinath	12	30	1	
Daryll Cullinan	b Kumble	55	74	7	
*Hansie Cronje	c Dravid b Kumble	18	30	2	
Brian McMillan	not out	59	76	6	
Shaun Pollock	not out	40	76	3	
†Dave Richardson					
Allan Donald					
Paul Adams					
Extras	(4 b, 12 lb, 1 w)	17			
Total	(6 wickets declared, 72 overs)	256			

Fall of wickets: 1-6 (Kirsten), 2-7 (Bacher), 3-33 (Klusener), 4-127 (Cullinan), 5-133 (Hudson), 6-155 (Cronje)

India bowling: Srinath 18-5-78-3, Ganesh 10-3-38-1, Prasad 7-1-16-0, Kumble 25-4-58-2, Ganguly 2-0-5-0, Raman 10-0-45-0

MATCH SCORECARD

India	Second innings		B	4	6
W.V. Raman	c Richardson b Pollock	16	48	1	
†Nayan Mongia	b Donald	2	17		
Rahul Dravid	c Richardson b Adams	12	48	1	
Sourav Ganguly	c McMillan b Pollock	30	82	5	
*Sachin Tendulkar	c Klusener b McMillan	9	28	1	
Mohammad Azharuddin	c Hudson b Donald	2	4		
VVS Laxman	not out	35	109	4	
Anil Kumble	c Richardson b Adams	14	45	1	
Dodda Ganesh	b Donald	1	7		
Venkatesh Prasad	st Richardson b Adams	15	16	2	
Javagal Srinath	absent ill				
Extras	(1 lb, 5 nb, 2 w)	8			
Total	(all out, 66.2 overs)	144			

Fall of wickets	1-7 (Mongia), 2-26 (Raman), 3-44 (Dravid), 4-59 (Tendulkar), 5-61 (Azharuddin), 6-87 (Ganguly), 7-115 (Kumble), 8-121 (Ganesh), 9-144 (Prasad)
South Africa bowling	Donald 18-5-40-3, Pollock 12-2-29-2, Klusener 9-3-13-0, McMillan 11-4-16-1, Adams 16.2-4-45-3

Umpires	Darrell Hair, Rudi Koertzen
TV umpire	Cyril Mitchley
Match referee	Barry Jarman
South Africa won by 282 runs	
Player of the Match	Brian McMillan

Day 1	SA 280/4 (90)
Day 2	SA 529/7d (162.5), India 29/3 (16)
Day 3	SA 529/7d (162.5) and 24/2 (12), Ind 359 (92.2)
Day 4	SA 529/7d (162.5) and 256/6d (72), Ind 359 (92.2) and 52/3 (28)
Day 5	SA 529/7d (162.5) and 256/6d (72), Ind 359 (92.2) and 144 (66.2)

Appendix

All facts and figures used in the book have been updated to August 2020 (the end of the Test series between England and Pakistan).

INDIA IN SOUTH AFRICA, 1996/97 (OTHER TEST MATCHES)

First Test: Kingsmead, Durban, 26–28 December 1996

South Africa 235 (A. Hudson 80; V. Prasad 5-60, J. Srinath 2-36) and 259 (A Bacher 55, A Hudson 52, B McMillan 51*; V Prasad 5-93, J. Srinath 3-80) beat **India** 100 (A. Donald 5-40, S. Pollock 2-18) and 66 (A. Donald 4-14, S. Pollock 3-25) by 328 runs.

Player of the Match: Andrew Hudson.

Third Test: New Wanderers, Johannesburg, 16–20 January 1997

India 410 (R. Dravid 148, S. Ganguly 73; L. Klusener 3-75, A. Donald 3-88) and 266/8 dec. (R. Dravid 81, S. Ganguly 60, N. Mongia 50; A. Donald 3-38, P. Adams 3-80) drew with **South Africa** 321 (S. Pollock 79, B. McMillan 47; J. Srinath 5-104, S. Ganguly 2-36) and 228/8 (D. Cullinan 122*, L. Klusener 49; A. Kumble 3-40, V. Prasad 2-59).

Player of the Match: Rahul Dravid.

Player of the Series: Allan Donald.

STANDARD BANK INTERNATIONAL ONE-DAY SERIES 1996/97 (SOUTH AFRICA, INDIA, ZIMBABWE)

South Africa won all their matches en route to the final. In the other matches, India and Zimbabwe won once each, while the other was a tie. India qualified on a better net run rate.

The final was abandoned due to rain. At that point South Africa had scored 42/1 in 14.3 overs in response to India's 191/9. South Africa won the reserve final by 44 runs. They put up 278/8 before bowling out India for 234.

Bibliography

Allen, David Rayvern, *Arlott: The Authorised Biography* (Harper Collins, 1996)

Arlott, John, *Alletson's Innings* (Epworth Press, 1958)

Bacher, Ali and Williams, David, *Jacques Kallis and 12 Other Great South African All-Rounders* (Penguin Global, 2014)

Bandyopadhyay, Kausik, *Mahatma on the Pitch: Gandhi & Cricket in India* (Rupa Publications India, 2017)

Barlow, Eddie, *Eddie Barlow: The Autobiography* (Tafelberg, 2006)

Bassano, Brian and Smith, Rick, *The Visit of Mr WW Read's 1891–92 English Cricket Team to South Africa* (JW McKenzie, 2007)

Bassano, Brian and Smith, Rick, *Vic's Boys in South Africa 1935–36* (Apple Books, 1993)

Bassano, Brian, *South African Cricket 1947–1960* (Cricket Connections International, 1996)

Benaud, Richie, *A Tale of Two Tests with Some Thoughts on Captaincy* (Hodder and Stoughton, 1962)

Bose, Mihir, *A History of Indian Cricket* (André Deutsch, 2002)

Bowen, Rowland, *Cricket: A History of its Growth and Development throughout the World* (Eyre and Spottiswoode, 1970)

Briggs, Paddy, *John Shepherd: The Loyal Cavalier* (ACS, 2009)

Brittenden, RT, *Silver Fern on the Veld* (AH & AW Reed, Wellington, 1954)

Buruma, Ian, *Playing the Game* (Farrar, Straus and Giroux, 1999)

Buskes, JJ, *Zuid-Afrika's Apartheidsbeleid: Onaanvaardbaar* (Bert Bakker, Daamen NV, 1955)

Chalke, Stephen, *Five Five Five: Holmes and Sutcliffe in 1932* (Fairfield Books, 2007)

Chalke, Stephen and Wells, Bryan, *One More Run: Gloucestershire Versus Yorkshire, Cheltenham 1957* (Fairfield Books, 2000)

Cox, Charles (ed), *The Cricketing Record of Major Warton's Tour 1888–89* (John McKenzie, 1987)

Crowley, Brian, *A Cavalcade of International Cricketers* (Pan Macmillan, 1988)

Crowley, Brian, *Currie Cup Story* (Don Nelson, 1973)

D'Oliveira, Basil, *D'Oliveira: An Autobiography* (Collins, 1968)

D'Oliveira, Basil, *The Basil D'Oliveira Affair* (Collins, 1969)

D'Oliveira, Basil, *Time to Declare: An Autobiography* (JM Dent & Sons, 1980)

D'Oliveira, John, *Vorster – the Man* (Ernest Stanton, 1977)

de Villiers, AB, *AB: The Autobiography* (Pan Macmillan, 2016)

Donald, Allan, *White Lightning* (Willow, 1999)

Duffus, Louis, *Play Abandoned: An Autobiography* (Howard Timmins, 1969)

Duffus, Louis, *South African Cricket 1927–1947* (South African Cricket Association, 1947)

Fingleton, Jack, *The Greatest Test of All* (Collins, 1961)

Frith, David, *Silence of the Heart* (Mainstream Publishing, 2001)

Gavaskar, Sunil, *One-day Wonders* (Rupa, 1986)

Gemmell, John, *The Politics of South African Cricket* (Routledge, 2004)

Ghosh, Mayukh, *In a League of their Own* (CricketMASH, 2019)

Goddard, Trevor, *Caught in the Deep* (Vision Media, 1988)

Grundling, Albert; Odendaal, André and Burridge, Spies, *Beyond the Tryline: Rugby and South African Society* (Ravan Press, 1995)

Guha, Ramachandra, *A Corner of a Foreign Field: The Indian History of a British Sport* (Picador, 2003)

Haigh, Gideon, *The Summer Game: Cricket and Australia in the 50s and 60s* (ABC Books, 2006)

Hain, Peter, *Don't Play with Apartheid* (George Allen & Unwin Ltd, 1971)

Hain, Peter, *Mandela: His Essential Life* (Rowman & Littlefield, 2018)

Heald, Tim, *Denis Compton: The Authorised Biography of the Incomparable* (Trafalgar Square, 1996)

Jenkinson, Neil, *C.B. Llewellyn: A Study in Equivocation* (ACS Publications, 2012)

Joffe, Joel, *The Rivonia Story* (Mayibuye, 1995)

Joffe, Joel, *The State vs Nelson Mandela* (Oneworld, 2007)

Keating, Frank, *Another Bloody Day in Paradise* (André Deutsch, 1981)

Laker, Jim, *Cricket Contrasts* (Stanley Paul, 1985)

Laker, Jim, *Over to Me* (Frederick Muller, 1960)

Laxman, VVS and Kaushik, R, *281 and Beyond* (Amazon Publishing, 2018)

Lazenby, John, *Edging Towards Darkness: The Story of the Last Timeless Test* (Wisden, 2017)

Lloyd, Grahame, *Howzat? The Six Sixes Ball Mystery* (Celluloid Ltd, 2013)

Lloyd, Grahame, *Six of the Best: Cricket's Most Famous Over* (Celluloid Ltd, 2008)

Luckin, M.W., *South African Cricket 1919–1927* (MW Luckin, 1927)

Luckin, M.W., *The History of South African Cricket* (WE Hortor & Co, 1915)

Majumdar, Boria, *Eleven Gods and a Billion Indians: The On and Off the Field Story of Cricket in India and Beyond* (Simon & Schuster India, 2018)

Manjrekar, Sanjay, *Imperfect* (HarperCollins India, 2017)

Manley, Michael and Symonds, Donna, *A History of West Indies Cricket* (André Deutsch, 2002)

Marchant, John, *The Greatest Test Match* (Faber & Gwyer, 1926)

May, Peter, *The Rebel Tours* (Sports Books, 2009)

Morris, Michael, *Apartheid* (Jonathan Ball, 2004)

Murray, Bruce and Merrett, Christopher, *Caught Behind: Race and Politics in Springbok Cricket* (Wits University Press, 2004)

Murray, Bruce; Parry, Richard and Winch, Jonty (ed), *Cricket and Society in South Africa 1910–1971* (Palgrave, Macmillan, 2018)

Oborne, Peter, *Basil D'Oliveira: Cricket and Conspiracy: The Untold Story* (Little, Brown, 2004)

Odendaal, André; Reddy, Krish and Merrett, Christopher, *Divided Country: The History of South African Cricket Retold 1914–1950s* (BestRed, 2018)

Odendaal, André; Reddy Krish; Merrett, Christopher and Winch, Jonty, *Cricket and Conquest: The History of South African Cricket Retold 1795–1914* (BestRed, 2016)

Odendaal, André, *The Story of an African Game* (David Phillip, 2003)

O'Sullivan, David, *The Extraordinary Book of South African Cricket* (Penguin Books South Africa, 2012)

Patel, J.M. Framjee, *Stray Thoughts on Indian Cricket* (Times Press, 1905)

Pearson, Harry, *Connie: The Marvellous Life of Learie Constantine* (Abacus, 2018)

Pollock, Peter, *Clean Bowled* (Vision Media, 1985)

Pollock, Peter, *God's Fast Bowler*, (Christian Art Publishers, 2001)

Procter, Mike, *South Africa: The Years of Isolation* (Queen Anne Press, 1994)

Procter, Mike and Zama, Lungani, *Caught in the Middle* (Don Nelson, 2017)

Purandare, Vaibhav, *Sachin Tendulkar: A Definitive Biography* (Lotus, 2005)

Raiji, Vasant, *India's Hambledon Men* (Tyeby Press, 1986)

Riley, John, *10th wicket First Class Cricket Record Partnership: 307 Runs: A.F. Kippax and J.E.H. Hooker, New South Wales, December 25th and 26th 1928* (Orchard Printing, 1997)

Ross, Alan, *Cape Summer and The Australians in England* (Constable, 1986)

Ross, Alan, *West Indies at Lord's* (Faber & Faber, 1963)

Sen, Ronojoy, *Nation at Play: A History of Sport in India* (Columbia University Press, 2015)

Sengupta, Arunabha, *Apartheid: A Point to Cover* (CricketMASH, 2020)

Short, Graham, *The Trevor Goddard Story* (Purfleet Productions, 1965)

Tendulkar, Sachin and Majumdar, Boria, *Playing it My Way* (Hodder & Stoughton, 2015)

Thompson, Leonard, *A History of South Africa* (Yale University Press, 1990)

van der Bijl, Vintcent, *Cricket in the Shadows* (Shuter & Shooter, 1984) van Ryneveld, Clive, *20th Century All-rounder* (Pretext, 2011)

Wagg, Stephen (ed), *Cricket and Nationality in the Postcolonial Age* (Routledge, 2005)

Warner, P.F., *The MCC in South Africa* (Chapman and Hall, 1906)

Waters, Chris, *10 for 10: Hedley Verity and the Story of Cricket's Greatest Bowling Feat* (Bloomsbury, 2014)

Welsh, David, *The Rise and Fall of Apartheid* (Jonathan Ball, 2009)

Welsh, Frank, *A History of South Africa* (Harper Collins, 2000)

Whimpress, Bernard, *W.G. Grace at Kadina: Champion Cricketer or Scoundrel?* (Flinders Press, 1994)

Woodward, Ian, *Sam Morris: Cricket's Capital All-Rounder* (Woodwards Pty Ltd, 2009)

Wright, John and Ugra, Sharda, *John Wright's Indian Summers* (Souvenir Press Limited, 2007)

Ananthanarayanan, N., *Why Sachin Tendulkar hated to face Hansie Cronje*, (https://www.hindustantimes.com/cricket/why-sachin-tendulkar-hated-to-face-hansie-cronje/story-IbrKlx7NKYfaE6Hd0GzqpM.html)

Brijnath, Rohit and Agarwal, Amit, *Doordarshan's intransigent attitude sends the Hero Cup for a six*, (https://www.indiatoday.in/magazine/sport/story/19931130-doordarshan-intransigent-attitude-sends-the-hero-cup-for-a-six-811887-1993-11-30)

Chidananda, Shreedutta, *Young Players need equal opportunities: Jonty Rhodes*, (https://www.thehindu.com/sport/cricket/young-black-players-need-equal-opportunity-jonty-rhodes/article30595640.ece)

Craddock, Robert, *Nelson Mandela didn't have to learn to play cricket to shape its destiny*, (https://www.dailytelegraph.com.au/sport/cricket/craddock-nelson-mandela-didnt-

have-to-learn-to-play-cricket-to-shape-its-destiny/
news-story/e933fa8a47956660f8b85448cf1a2809)
Date, Kartikeya, *Headingley 2019*, (https://cricketingview.
substack.com/p/headingley-2019)
Davis, Charles, *Z-score's Cricket Stats Blog*, (http://www.
sportstats.com.au/)
Lokapally, Vijay, *Sunil Gavaskar: I would've been a
doctor if not a cricketer*, (https://sportstar.thehindu.
com/magazine/sunil-gavaskar-interview-career-life-
pataudi-1983-world-cup-gaekwad-vengsarkar-sobers-
viswanath-viv-richards-sacin-sehwag-ranji-india/
article29787100.ece)
Viswanath, G., *Tendulkar's 169 at Cape Town is one of the
greatest: Bacher* (https://www.thehindu.com/sport/cricket/
tendulkars-169-at-cape-town-is-one-of-the-greatest-
bacher/article7843128.ece)
Williamson, Martin, *The Denness Affair*, (https://www.
espncricinfo.com/magazine/content/story/496743.
html)

Wisden Almanacks
Wikipedia
ESPNCricinfo
CricketCountry
Cricmash
YouTube
Sportstar
India Today
The Hindu

Index

Botham, Ian 143-4, 148, 166
Boult, Trent 148-9
Boycott, Geoff 19, 72
Bradman, Don 19, 74, 96, 100, 129, 133-4, 163
Brittain-Jones, Jack 94
Broad, Chris 72, 121-2
Broad, Stuart 37, 148
Bumrah, Jasprit 152
Buruma, Ian 128
Caddick, Andy 183
Cairns, Lance 148-9
Chalke, Stephen 10, 17, 18
Chappell, Greg 133, 218
Chappell, Trevor 88
Chatfield, Ewen 148
Chauhan, Chetan 161, 166-7
Cheetham, Jack 74-5
Chevalier, Graham 69
Clark, 'Nobby' 162
Clarke, Michael 134, 208
Clarke, Sylvester 72, 75-6, 105
Close, Brian 19, 24, 72
Compton, Denis 103, 228-9
Constantine, Lebrun 92
Cook, Jimmy 12, 70, 72, 77, 113
Cowdrey, Colin 17, 20, 80
Croft, Colin 72, 75-7
Cronje, Hansie 26, 37, 39-40, 108, 139-41, 146-7, 177-9, 187
Crowe, Martin 188
Crowley, Brian 89
Cullinan, Daryll 13, 33, 54-5, 193, 198
D'Oliveira, Basil 38-40, 43, 67-8, 85, 89, 95, 116, 118, 227

Dakin, Geoff 119
Dalmiya, Jagmohan 45, 215-17, 219
Das, Shiv Sundar 212, 214, 220
Dasgupta, Deep 174, 212, 214
Date, Kartikeya 195
de Klerk, F.W. 112, 119, 122-4
de Lange, Marchant 211
de Silva, Aravinda 58, 118
de Villiers, A.B. 224, 232
de Villiers, Dawie 185
de Villiers, Fanie 66, 70, 151
de Wet, Quartus 99
Denness, Mike 212-22
Dev, Kapil 12, 23, 60, 62-3, 143, 152, 154, 167, 202, 206
Deve Gowda, H.D. 48
Dhoni, M.S. 170, 174
Dillon, Mervyn 195
Divecha, 'Buck' 192
Donald, Allan 12, 26, 36, 37, 53, 56-7, 60, 70, 72, 77-9, 86, 97, 107-9, 134-8, 147-8, 150-1, 153, 155, 157, 177-80, 182-4, 198, 206-7
Dravid, Rahul 27, 29, 33-4, 54-6, 62, 161, 169, 181, 188-90, 198-201, 211, 219, 221
du Plessis, Faf 223, 231
Duffus, Louis 85
Duleepsinhji, Kumar Shri 94, 125
Dyson, John 72
Edrich, John 19, 24
Ellison, Richard 72, 121
Emburey, John 72, 122
Faulkner, Aubrey 38-9, 95
Fleetwood-Smith, 'Chuck' 102

INDEX

About the authors

Arunabha Sengupta is a cricket historian, analyst and writer for numerous cricket publications. He is the author of *Apartheid: A Point to Cover – South African cricket 1948–1970 and the Stop The Seventy Tour.*

He also wrote the cricket-based Sherlock Holmes pastiche *Sherlock Holmes and the Birth of The Ashes.*

Cricket historian, analyst and writer **Abhishek Mukherjee** was the chief editor of *CricketCountry* and assistant editor of *Wisden India Almanack.* He has written for many other cricket publications.

Also available at all good book stores

9781785316395

9781785317224

9781785315053

9781785314865

9781785314377

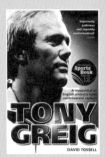

9781785313981

9781785314070

9781785313806

9781785317217